Pure Heart

Pure Heart

A SPIRITED TALE OF
GRACE, GRIT, AND WHISKEY

Troy Ball
WITH BRET WITTER

DEY ST.
An Imprint of WILLIAM MORROW

DEY ST.

HarperCollins books may be purchased for educational, business, or sales promotional use. For information, please email the Special Markets Department at SPsales@harpercollins.com.

FIRST EDITION

Designed by Paula Russell Szafranski

Library of Congress Cataloging-in-Publication Data
Names: Ball, Troylyn, 1959- author. | Witter, Bret, author.
Title: Pure heart : a spirited tale of grace, grit, and whiskey / Troylyn Ball with Bret Witter.
Description: First edition. | New York, NY : Dey Street, [2017] | Includes bibliographical references.
Identifiers: LCCN 2016047421| ISBN 9780062458971 (hardcover) | ISBN 9780062458988 (pbk.) | ISBN 9780062660602 (audio) | ISBN 9780062458964 (e-book)
Subjects: LCSH: Ball, Troylyn, 1959- | Distillers—United States—Biography. | Whiskey industry—North Carolina. | Whiskey—North Carolina. | Real estate developers—United States--Biography. | Caregivers—United States—Biography.
Classification: LCC HD9395.U47 B355 2017 | DDC 338.4/766352092 [B] --dc23 LC record available at https://lccn.loc.gov/2016047421

17 18 19 20 21   RRD   10 9 8 7 6 5 4 3 2 1

TO MY MOTHER, LOUISE,

AND TO MARSHALL FOR TEACHING ME

WHAT A PURE HEART IS

Note: The quotations that begin each section are from my son Marshall Ball and his book Kiss of God.

UNDERSTANDING TAKES A

DEAR GOOD LISTENING THINKER.

CONTENTS

What Is Pure Heart?

QUESTION: IS WISDOM BORN OF EXPERIENCE,

OR CAN IT BE LEARNED BY READING A BOOK?

ANSWER: WISDOM KNOWS MANY ANSWERS,

BUT LISTENING IS NEEDED.

Some people say if you don't live your dreams when you're young, you never will. You'll end up settling. Working a job just for a paycheck. Marrying someone you don't truly love. Cooking dinner every night. (Sorry, but I don't like cooking.) You'll never take that wild business chance or that Alaskan cruise. You'll never have that crazy affair of the heart. You'll wake up one day, realize you're past your prime, and think, *Why didn't I take the chance? Why didn't I live when I was young and I didn't have all these sore muscles and responsibilities?* Once you think that, they say, it's already too late.

There was a time I thought that way, too. After twenty-four years of being a stay-at-home mother, I thought life had passed me by. I would sit in my house, exhausted, and think back on my childhood in rural Texas, when my father would sit with me at the end of a day spent working and ask me, "What do you want to do, Troy?"

I knew the answer. I wanted to be a wife and mother, have a big family, the usual stuff. But I also wanted to be an entrepreneur. I wanted to run my own business, just like Dad.

"Well, how you gonna make that happen, Troy?" Dad would say as we watched the beautiful Texas sunset. He wasn't patronizing me. He really wanted to know.

Even at ten, I knew the answer, because Dad had taught me well. I would go to college. I would get a good job and learn a business. I would look for an opportunity, a hole in the market nobody else had seen, and I'd fill that hole with whatever was missing from the world. Then I'd sell it. I'd sell the product, the idea, the service. I'd sell them on myself. I didn't know what my business would be. Maybe horses. I loved horses as a girl. (Still do.) Or maybe insurance, because that was Dad's primary business. It didn't matter, because what I wanted was to create something of my own. Be the boss. Sell. Succeed. I imagined sitting on a front porch, just like my childhood porch, when I was an older woman (which to my ten-year-old self probably meant forty). I'd have my handsome husband beside me, my kids and grandkids around me, and hundreds of friends spreading over my little corner of the world, laughing and carrying on. And I'd be in the center, the queen, because my business would have provided for them all.

It didn't work out that way. I got the handsome husband and sons, but I had to give up my entrepreneurial dreams, and for twenty-four years my life felt small. For a while, it felt like my world shrank every year, until it was just me, in my house, by myself, taking care of my three boys, two of whom had special needs. And the smaller my life got, the harder it was to hold it together, and the more down on myself I became. On my worst days, I resented my husband, my sons, the friends who had left me behind. I felt lonely, and I felt guilty about that loneliness, because I knew I should have been happy living for my family, because my family needed me, and they loved me, and how could I be angry about that?

Then, in my late forties, I found my hole to fill in the last place I ever would have looked. I found it in moonshine.

I'm probably not who you think of when you think of a moonshiner. I don't have a name like Willie Carter Sharpe . . . Okay, I guess Troylyn Wigginton Ball is pretty close. But I don't have Willie's childhood in the Appalachian Mountains, or her teenage years working in an overall factory, or her diamond-studded teeth. That was the detail that caught America's attention when Willie Carter Sharpe went on trial in 1935 for running carloads of illegal 'shine two or three times a day, three hundred sixty-five days a year, for ten years. More than enough runs, at $10 a pop, to pay for any kind of teeth she wanted.

I'm from Texas. I grew up comfortable, first in the suburbs, then on a ranch. I've always lived in good houses in nice neighborhoods. I wear boots, but the fashionable kind, and I always wear my pearls. If you saw me, you'd probably think I was just another nice Southern wife, with an SUV and a lunch date at the Junior League. You'd almost be right. But I never joined the Junior League, and truth be told, I was never going to be happy lunching with the ladies.

And that's where my road and Willie Carter Sharpe's meet. When the reporters asked her why she ran 'shine, Willie said, "It was the excitement got me."

It was the excitement of white whiskey—a.k.a. white lightning, a.k.a. mountain dew, a.k.a. moonshine—that got me, too. As soon as an old mountain man handed me a mason jar of the "keeper 'shine," as he called it, I wanted to learn everything about it. I wanted to make it, then make it legal. Shoot-outs with the law, Willie said, made her feel alive. For me, it was

realizing that real moonshine wasn't rotgut garbage. Traditional Scotch-Irish Appalachian moonshine had a history that
dated back long before Prohibition, and it was one of the best
hard liquors the world had ever known.

And nobody, anywhere, was making it that way anymore.
When I discovered that, I knew moonshine was my opportu-
nity. It was going to be my business and my adventure. I guess
I hoped moonshine would save my soul.

Then my world collapsed, and moonshine had to save my
family, too.

"Pure heart" is a whiskey-making term. The start of a distillation (known as a run) is filled with poisons that burn off at
low temperatures. That's the heads. The end of a run is full of
greasy heavy oils that burn off at high temperatures. That's the
tails. The center of the run, where the temperature is perfect, is
called the heart, because the spirit found there is pure and clear.

When I learned this, I vowed to throw the heads and tails
away, so that my moonshine was nothing but pure heart. I've
done that since the first bottle of Troy & Sons, and I still do
that today. Every drop of Troy & Sons whiskey is pure heart,
guaranteed.

I also vowed to incorporate that concept into my daily life.
Every decision I make, whether for my business or my family,
I try to make with a pure heart. I throw away the light poisons
of shortcuts and half-truths. I throw out the heavy poisons of
anger, fear, and resentment. I try to do what's right, because
when you are drinking (and thinking) from a pure heart, you'll
never regret your actions the next morning.

So please, sit back with a "spiderleg" of Troy & Sons heirloom moonshine, as my great friend Forrest Jarrett would say,
and relax. Have two spiderlegs, actually, because as Forrest is
fond of saying, while holding out his cup, "Bird can't fly with

one wing, so best give me two." He's a man not afraid to mix metaphors, or a stiff drink.

Not a straight whiskey drinker? Here's a favorite cocktail recipe:

> 1½ oz Troy & Sons Platinum heirloom moonshine
>
> ½ oz fresh-squeezed orange juice
>
> 1½ oz fresh-squeezed lime juice
>
> ¾ to 1 oz simple syrup (half sugar, half water, mixed and dissolved), depending on how sweet you want the drink

Or just have lemonade. I don't drink much myself. I had my first taste of alcohol, a glass of red wine, when I was forty years old, so this isn't a drinking story, anyway. It's a story about pursuing your passion, no matter how old you are or how high the mountain in the way. Whether I sell another bottle of moonshine, or make another dollar, doesn't matter. I've helped the people I needed to help, and I've loved the people who gave me their time and talent, and I've found my life's purpose in the trying.

I guess that's the pure heart of this story, too.

PART I

Listener's Hill

HAPPINESS BEGINS WHEN
WE AGREE TO LOVE.

EACH DAY THE ANSWERS COME
TO A GOOD DEAR LISTENER.

MAKE EACH DAY A HAPPY ONE
AND GO TO A GOOD GOD.

CHAPTER 1

BEFORE MARSHALL

My dad was a scrapper. I mean that metaphorically, although he may, for all I know, have sorted scrap metal as a kid. He did just about every other job imaginable, since he was born right before the stock market crashed in 1929, the seventh child of a poor family from the outskirts of Palestine, Texas. He grew up during the Depression, eating barely enough to live on and wearing clothes made out of potato sacks. He didn't talk until he was three, but once he started, he never stopped. He was going to make a fortune through hard work and smarts, he said, and nothing was going to stop him. He married young, when he was still a field hand. Eventually, he worked his way into the grocery business. By the time he was in his early twenties, he was a divorced father with a partial college education but a solid career as a food broker. He wooed my mother, whom he met at a church picnic, with the olives he was selling to local grocers and restaurants.

They married when Mom was nineteen and soon had me. Mom named me Troylyn, partially because it sounded like a strong boy's name and partially to honor her Greek father. I've always gone by Troy. Troy Wigginton for the first twenty-three years of my life. My name made it sound like I was destined to be a small-town Texas quarterback. I wasn't.

I was destined to be my father's daughter, and Dad couldn't have cared less about sports. Or politics. Or most of the other things people found entertaining. Dad was an entrepreneur. His passion was starting businesses. He loved the rush of taking an idea from nothing to something, of selling the public on a service or product that hadn't existed before.

That's what made Dad extraordinary: he believed in the power of selling. He read about selling. He studied it. Other fathers took their seven-year-old daughters to patty-cake parties or softball games; Dad took me to Zig Ziglar sales seminars.

"If you know how to sell," he drummed into me, "you will always survive. No matter what happens, Troy, you will always be able to take care of yourself."

Dad never mixed with the high-class crowd. He was a poor kid at heart, and he never cared about social graces, no matter how much money he had. He hated the idea of playing people off each other or lying to get ahead. He wouldn't join a country club or even own golf clubs, even though the golf course was where business connections were made. He turned down invitations to fancy parties. He never drank or smoked, and he never gambled, except on his own business ideas. Dad was average height, but he was strong and barrel-chested, and he had a huge personality. He was always selling, and part of that was selling his children on his way of life.

I remember him calling for my younger brother and me one

evening after work. I must have been eight, which would have made my brother seven. Dad had ten tickets to AstroWorld, an amusement park in Houston reputed among my friends to be the greatest place on earth.

"I got these free at the office," he said. "Why don't you take them around the neighborhood and try to sell them? I'll let you keep the money."

You know how the story ends, right? The two enthusiastic children sell the tickets. Dad lets them keep the money. Then he takes them to AstroWorld.

Except it didn't happen that way. We kept the money from our sales, but Dad never took us to AstroWorld. (Mom took us later, though.) Maybe it was those kinds of disappointments that eventually pushed some of my siblings away from Dad. I had a brother, two sisters, and an older half sister from Dad's first marriage. They weren't comfortable with our father's intensity and expectations. Some eventually had problems with him, and one grew to despise him.

I idolized my dad. *Idolized* him. I ate up every word of advice he ever gave me, even when I was no higher than his Texas-sized belt buckle. If Dad said sell, I sold.

Dad didn't own the food brokerage. That was just a job. His first business was a billboard company. Then he founded an insurance business. Not an insurance office, but a whole company. He didn't hit it big, though, until the early 1970s, when I was twelve or thirteen years old. Dad loved rushing into new ventures, but he wasn't much for the drudgery of slowly building profits. He probably made a few fortunes in those early years, but he'd take what he earned and plow it into a new business, and he lost exactly as many fortunes as he gained. Dad didn't care. *As long as you can sell, no matter how broke you are at the moment, you'll be fine in the end.*

Then Dad put in a bid for the last radio license available in the city of Houston. The government owned the license, and at least in theory, they were legally required to issue it to the person who would best serve the public interest. The other bidders had more experience and money, not to mention better contacts, but Dad had something they didn't: a good idea. They wanted to play music. Dad wanted to start the first all-news radio station in Texas. To the surprise of just about everyone but himself, Dad was granted the license. It had taken him seven years of work.

The very next day (or so it seems in my memory), he went out and started selling advertising for the station. Have I mentioned that Dad could sell?

"If they say no," he told me, "that's just because they don't have enough information yet, so keep talking until they say yes."

The radio station was a success, so Dad moved the family from Houston to a dusty ranch in the rolling hill country thirty miles away. He bought a few head of cattle (for show) and a mile-long Lincoln. Soon after, he came home wearing a ring with a yellow diamond so big it made my eyes pop. (God, I wish I had that ring now.) Mom, on the other hand, was the quintessential 1960s Texas housewife: washing, cooking, taking care of everyone. She said being married to Don Wigginton was like living in the shade of an oak tree.

Mom was right. Dad was a hundred feet tall and impervious to storms. In Dad's shadow, Mom's lovely qualities seemed to disappear.

He was my hero. Dad woke up every morning at seven to work on projects, mostly ideas for new businesses or manual labor on the ranch. He made all his children wake up to help him. Even I grumbled when I heard "Sun's up, day's a-wasting," but that didn't keep me from working until I dropped.

By twelve, I was following Dad on sales calls. By fourteen, I was doing office work at the insurance company—filing, mailing form letters, that kind of thing. At fifteen, I started selling radio advertising. I had to generate my own leads, but Dad was always planting seeds.

"I saw you looking at that necklace in the jewelry store," he said. "If you go sell them some ads, they might give you a discount."

Yes sir, Dad. It only took me a few months to buy that necklace, on discount (because I was selling myself to them too) and paid for with my cut of their advertising account.

"You're sixteen now," Dad said a year later. "I know every sixteen-year-old wants a car. I want a big ad campaign from the Pontiac dealer. You think there's a way to work something out?"

It took a bit longer than a few months for that one, but I earned a Pontiac, too.

Two years later, I left for college. The guidance counselor at Sealy High School in Sealy, Texas, told me there were three choices for kids from our small town: the University of Texas, Texas A&M, or the local community college.

I chose Texas A&M, where a few months before the end of my freshman year I met a senior named Charlie. Oh boy, was he good-looking. With his square jaw and wavy hair, he looked like Kurt Russell. And he was likable. That's the thing about Charlie: everybody loves him. He's not that talkative (compared to me), but put him in a group, and after a few months, everybody in that group will consider him their best friend.

Charlie was my first love, and our relationship was serious immediately, even though he was graduating. We were so serious that Charlie and I discussed together what he'd do after college, and I told him to take the job in Singapore being offered by a major engineering firm. Southeast Asia was deep in a huge wave of infrastructure projects like bridges, and civil engineers there were being paid twice the starting salary of a job in the United States. If Charlie went overseas for a few years and saved his money, he'd come home with a nice nest egg.

So we said our good-byes. Charlie went to Asia and I, finally realizing the world was bigger than Texas, transferred to Vanderbilt University in Nashville, Tennessee. I don't know if you're familiar with the popular image of the Vanderbilt girl. She takes pride in being smart, friendly, well dressed (conservative but fashionable), approachable, and well behaved . . . most of the time. She has a nice smile, and she uses it. She has good manners. She's pretty, but not *too* pretty. Ambitious, but not so you'd notice, at least not right away.

Well, I'm a Vanderbilt girl. I love pressed blue jeans and nice blouses, and I almost never go out without my hair done and my pearl earrings. I was raised very religious. I didn't drink, and I've never smoked. I pride myself on my Southern manners. But that doesn't mean I don't have fun. I like people, and I like making friends, from my neighbors to the owner of my favorite Thai restaurant, who always greets me with a hug.

And I've always been ambitious. At Vandy, I graduated in three years and was the manager of the student newspaper. I met and became engaged to a brilliant PhD student from a good family. I was accepted into the business school. I wanted to be an entrepreneur like Dad, and I knew Vanderbilt's business school would give me the necessary connections.

But Dad wanted me back in Texas. He wanted me to be his protégée, and he wanted me by his side. Even an oak tree, after all, needs someone to sit underneath its branches and look up in wonder. I had always been the one to most admire his reach and celebrate his strength.

So I went home to Sealy, Texas, to get married and work with Dad. The month before the wedding, Charlie, my old boyfriend from Texas A&M, showed up at Dad's office, where I worked. He was just back from Indonesia. We went into a room alone, and he paced the floor.

"I thought you were going to wait for me," he said.

"We agreed to see other people when you left. We broke up. You said we had to."

"I know. I thought you'd wait for me," he said. His head was down. He couldn't look at me. "I guess I'm not the marrying kind," he muttered sadly.

I was married to my Vanderbilt man the next month. I ran Dad's insurance marketing and then, for most of a year, managed his newest business, a sand mining operation, out of a trailer in the middle of the pit. Now, that's a dirty job. Loud, industrial, and 110 degrees, with grit flying all day into your nostrils, mouth, and every other place.

At night, I helped my husband research and write his energy investments newsletter. I thought he was my new partner, like Dad had always been, because he was brilliant. I loved his mind. But as I soon learned, he was also jealous, erratic, and prone to violence. He watched me, and everything I did was wrong. So he yelled at me. He hit me. One night, about a year into our marriage, he pushed me down the stairs.

I escaped to a friend's house and cried in her arms. I made excuses. My friend was older and more experienced than I was, and she wasn't having it. "Troy," she said, "if he treats you like this when you're young, imagine how he's going to treat you at forty. This won't get better."

She was right. I left him, even though he fought it, legally and otherwise.

And when I was free, I found out Charlie was still waiting.

He had stayed in touch with my parents, sending them gifts and Christmas cards, helping whenever they called. He really was the kind of man you should spend a life with—the marrying kind, as he had said. A year and a half later, in a small ceremony in our backyard, I married Charlie Ball, the man I should have waited for in the first place.

We moved to Austin, Texas, where Charlie had a job lined up as a project manager for a large developer. I got a job at Nash Phillips/Copus, a major homebuilder. I managed archaeological surveys, helped map residential developments, designed recreation areas, and worked with the state of Texas to preserve archaeological artifacts and sites discovered on Nash Phillips/Copus land. I loved the job. I loved Charlie. For a brief moment, everything was perfect. Everything was according to plan.

Then our son Marshall was born, and everything changed.

CHAPTER 2

MARSHALL

There's a reason people say the births of their children are the most important moments of their lives. What can compare to holding a life in your arms? A life you created, but a life that is free, existing near you, and dependent on you, though not yours.

The second you look at your baby for the first time, warm and damp and (probably) crying, you experience a new and deeper love than you've ever known. If you've been there, you know what I mean. If you haven't, take it from me, it's better than you've imagined. When I held Marshall, I felt as if my life was complete. I didn't need his perfect Apgar test (a measure of a baby's health at birth) to tell me he was perfect. I could see it in his pink skin, his round cheeks, his tiny fingers and toes.

I could see his life stretching before us. That is something else the birth of a child provides. I wanted to live forever in that first day in the hospital, when Marshall was tiny and in my arms. But as I looked at my baby, like all new mothers, I also saw the road ahead: learning to crawl, then walk, then talk; the first day of school; his first friend; teaching him to read, throw a baseball, and open a door for a girl. I saw graduation, a job, a wife, and eventually my grandchildren. Marshall's life would have its ups and downs, of course, but I already knew the general shape.

There were signs of trouble, but I explained them away, telling myself they were nothing to worry about. Marshall had difficulty breastfeeding, so I switched to formula. He was slow to gain weight, but that could have been for many reasons. Marshall was a human being, not a set of rules. He would find his way.

At five months, he began to have spasms. His body would tense suddenly, then relax. At six months, he weighed less than twelve pounds, and he still couldn't sit up on his own. I had planned to go back to work, but Marshall needed me, so I devoted myself to his care. I fed him. I changed him. I watched him, waiting for eye contact or a smile. I propped him on pillows to strengthen his back, read him books, moved toys in front of his face to get him to react.

There was something wrong. I knew it before the doctor told me. The spasms were getting worse, his tiny body seizing up and sending him into obvious discomfort. The doctor thought they were seizures, but he couldn't find a cause. I started to monitor everything Marshall did: when and what he ate, when and how much he slept. I cleaned the entire house and replaced anything that could have been causing him problems: his blankets, his toys, the laundry detergent.

I reviewed every decision, no matter how small, to think of what we'd done and what we could change. Had I eaten the wrong things during pregnancy? Exercised too much, or too little? Had we painted the walls with something toxic? Always, there was that nagging thought: what had I done to my little boy?

I spent every moment I could with Marshall, and when I slept, or simply gave out, Charlie was there. We were always vigilant, never sleeping more than a couple of hours at a stretch, because Marshall never slept more than that. My brain may have been foggy from sleep deprivation and worry, my heart may have been heavy with sadness, but I was determined. I was never going to give up, and I was never going to leave Marshall alone. I even volunteered at the church nursery, so that I could be with him. I watched the other babies grab things, laugh, and look into my eyes. At nine months, Marshall could only lie in my arms or on the carpet. He could barely hold up his head.

Every other child was advancing. Week after week, I watched babies younger than Marshall begin to crawl, and then to walk. I watched them begin to play with scooters and those popcorn-popper walkers. I saw them clap with excitement at their accomplishments. What was wrong with my son?

Nothing!

Everything.

I left the nursery every Sunday in tears.

It felt like a death. I had my baby boy, but those hopes—the first day of kindergarten, the T-ball games, the first girlfriend— were dying. I would see another child doing something ordinary, or I'd simply pass a school or playground, and suddenly I'd feel the loss. *Marshall will never have that. I'll never experience it with him.* I mean it sincerely; the pain was as sharp, for me, as the loss of my father when that came years later. It was the pain of knowing your loved one is gone forever. They will never walk through that door. For me, that loved one was the boy and the man I had imagined Marshall would be.

That didn't make me love Marshall less. In fact, it made me

love him more ferociously. I was more determined than ever to give my son whatever he needed to succeed, whatever that word meant for him now. That's something my Christian faith gave me: the ability to accept Marshall for the beauty of his spirit, regardless of the struggles of his body.

But I *was* disappointed: not with Marshall, but with life. I cried every night when, at a year old, he still couldn't hold anything in his hands. He could hook his finger around a string of Mardi Gras beads—I was so proud, we worked on it every day—but he never progressed further. Even after I became pregnant with our second son, Coulton, Charlie and I tracked everything Marshall ate, touched, looked at, or dropped. I charted the timing and intensity of his seizures. The doctor couldn't find any answers, but the answers had to be there. There had to be a reason for Marshall's condition. It was 1988. Serious medical problems didn't just go unexplained.

Coulton, like Marshall, was born perfect. He was smaller than his brother had been, but he was strong. Charlie and I prayed for him every day, we did everything the doctor asked of us, but he never gained weight. He was wobbly when he tried to lift his head. At four months, he started to have seizures, even worse than the ones Marshall had experienced. I can't say it was a crushing blow. I was so heartbroken by then that Coulton's seizures felt both devastating and inevitable.

I was raised in a strict Christian home. My mother was a regular in the church; Dad read his Bible every day. Our faith anchored the family; it has helped me greatly in life. It assures me that although my boys' bodies are damaged, their souls are pure. They exist in love. In all the important ways, my sons are whole.

But our religious teachings explicitly rejected modern medicine. My parents had bent when I took Marshall to regular doctor's visits, but my mother was devastated when I told her I was taking the boys to neurological specialists.

"Oh no, Troy," she cried. "No. No. You're manifesting the illness."

My parents believed that, because we are made in the image and likeness of God, it is our spirits, not our bodies, that need mending. To them, Marshall's and Coulton's conditions were a test of faith, to be treated not with medicine, but with study and prayer.

That teaching had a powerful hold on me. I believed it, too. But I couldn't let my sons suffer in this life without doing everything I could to help them, and that meant taking them to the best specialists in Austin, Texas, and beyond. That decision not only meant hurting my mother; it meant leaving the church that had nurtured my life. It would be hypocritical to profess my faith, I thought, if I wasn't willing to follow all the church's tenets. I had to hold true, or I had to leave.

Dad knew I was suffering. He knew the family was being torn apart. He took me aside. He didn't agree with what I was doing, but he told me: "This is your decision, Troy. I'm with you, always, whatever you decide."

Dad was a giving man. He had always loved and believed in me. But he was deeply religious. So I hadn't expected his blessing. The greatest gift Dad ever gave me was, at that moment, to hold me closer by letting me go.

I remember crying. Maybe Dad did, too. He reached out and hugged me, so that I could feel his love. Then he looked me in the face and said, "Troy, do you know what you need to do?" I nodded yes. "Then next time we talk, I want to hear that you did it."

CHAPTER 3

THE CAT

I'm still not sure going to see the specialist was a good idea. The causes of Marshall's and Coulton's condition were never determined, and no physical progress was ever made. The boys have genetic metabolic disorders, and their symptoms are probably the result of a cluster of undiagnosable conditions. They don't have muscular dystrophy, but that is the closest analogue. Neither Marshall nor Coulton has good control of his arms or legs, and neither is balanced enough to sit on his own without help. They spend most of their time lying on their backs, in my arms, or buckled into wheelchairs. They struggle to make facial expressions, and neither has ever been able to talk. Their muscles simply have never developed, leaving both of them just under five feet tall. Marshall currently weighs one hundred pounds, the largest he's ever been. Coulton weighs ninety pounds. They are thirty and twenty-eight years old.

Coulton's condition is more serious than Marshall's. In

addition to his physical problems, Coulton has severe autism. He can't maintain eye contact and often rocks back and forth. There were months when he hit himself on the head continually. At times, his only comfort is being tightly bound, for instance in a blanket. For more than a decade, he would only eat if the Barney theme song was playing. Once the music stopped, we had to start the recording again before he would take another bite. Eventually, getting enough nutrition into him became so difficult that we had to feed him liquid supplements through a port surgically implanted in his side.

I worry my decision to trust the neurologist might be partially to blame. (I worry. Period. All the time.) When I went to the specialist, I had two years' worth of carefully compiled information on Marshall's symptoms and environment. I was dedicated to my child; I *knew* him. I had heard that some families were experimenting with diet and environment to treat seizures. Might that be an option? I asked.

The neurologist dismissed my ideas and the information I'd gathered. He said these were medical conditions, and the boys needed a medical treatment. He prescribed Depakote, an anti-seizure medicine, for both boys. When the seizures decreased but didn't stop, he upped the dosage. Soon both boys were taking the maximum amount for their sizes. Marshall was two and a half, but Coulton was only six months old. We now know that Depakote can be harmful to infants, especially at high doses. It may even be linked to autism. Later, I learned our neurologist had been researching dosages of Depakote. He wasn't just treating my boys, but using them in a study. I was devastated. I gave up my religion to trust the medical community, and they hadn't been fully honest with me.

I've found this feeling of frustration and betrayal to be common among parents with special needs children. Severe autism, for instance, is a devastating diagnosis. The lack of information makes it harder. We want to know the physical cause—what broke down in my child?—but doctors can only say, "We don't know." Was the problem external? Was it preventable? Did we pass along something hidden in our genetic code? Am I *responsible*? "We don't know." As parents, we need to know why our children seem okay, sometimes for years, and then suddenly they aren't. More importantly, we want to know what we can do to help them. The response from doctors is the single worst word of all: "Nothing."

So we throw ourselves into finding answers. All the ambition I had to be an entrepreneur, all my energy and drive, went into my boys. All those hours I would have spent working at Nash Phillips/Copus or starting my own business, I devoted to making their lives better. The boys were zombies on the Depakote. The dosage was so high, they did nothing all day but stare unfocused into space, drooling down their chins. If this was the improved life modern medicine promised, it wasn't for us.

I researched frantically, looking for information and ideas. If there was anyone, anywhere, who had a new treatment or theory, I would go to them, and I would ask that doctor or clinic for referrals. I drove the boys all over the state of Texas. I drove them to neighboring states. I heard about a place in California, and since plane tickets were expensive and the boys couldn't really travel that way, I drove them more than twenty hours to the clinic. I drove them to Colorado. I talked to doctors from all over the world.

When Marshall was five, I was referred to the Environmental Health Center in Dallas. Every room at the center is sterile. No one is allowed to wear perfume, makeup, or body wash, and the rooms and hallways are cleaned daily with contaminant-free products. The boys spent three weeks there, being tested for allergies and other environmental factors. They had so many allergies it was disheartening, but I was determined to follow the center's recommendations.

I cleaned my house and kept it sterile. I started the boys on a strict dietary regimen and logged every bite they took. When I stopped giving them dairy products, their seizures improved, so I cut back on the dosage of Depakote. The neurologist was against it, but these weren't his children. The seizures didn't return, so I went further, cutting out carbohydrates and replacing them with plenty of fats and proteins. I prepared nine individual servings for each of them every morning, and I carried scales everywhere, because the small meals were weighed to the milligram and timed to the minute. The seizures slowed as their bodies cleansed, and I cut their Depakote again.

By the time I fully implemented the center's recommendations, their seizures had become so infrequent, and I was so well informed about how to care for them, that I weaned them off the Depakote entirely.

Not that there wasn't a trade-off. The Depakote kept the boys quiet and malleable. They slept for hours, and sometimes through the night. Understand, I had already lived through five years of suffering, twenty-four hours a day. The Depakote had made my life easier.

My new approach meant I was constantly working: cooking, cleaning, monitoring, charting, changing diapers, moving the boys to new positions, pushing them in their wheelchairs to get them fresh air. It's not that I would have been out having lunch with friends otherwise. When you have children as frail as Marshall and Coulton, you are terrified to leave them. I cannot count the number of times we rushed one of the boys to the hospital with a life-threatening lung infection or other illness. What if I wasn't there for them? What if I wasn't paying attention? The vigilance was my life. I never questioned it. Charlie and I had decided early on that we would cherish our time with the boys, and we would treat them like normal children. But because Charlie had a full-time job, the burden fell mostly on me.

Why is a whine, I would tell myself when the routine began to crush me. *This is for Marshall and Coulton. This is your duty. This is your blessing.*

Don't stop, Troy. You know what you need to do. So do it.

I read to the boys every day. I sang songs to them. I took them to the zoo, played them classical music (good for brain development, experts say), and kissed them as often as I could.

"I love you," I told them. "Marshall, Coulton, you are loved."

It was hard work. The boys had to be constantly monitored, even during the night, so Charlie and I never slept for more than a few hours at a time. We rarely went on dates. When we did, it was hard to have fun. I couldn't relax and be with my husband. The boys were always between us.

I have heard of men pulling away in this situation. They think, *I'm young. I'm in my early thirties. This isn't the life I signed up for.* Charlie was never like that. He never went out for a drink with the guys from work. He didn't play golf or fantasy sports. He knew we needed him, and he was dedicated to Coulton and Marshall. He came home from work and sang to them; he changed their diapers in the middle of the night. He carried them, which wasn't easy, despite their small size. I know he grieved. What father doesn't want to help his son take his first steps, to watch him run, to help him buy his first car? What father doesn't dream of his son discovering dreams of his own? Of course Charlie ached when he thought of those little deaths. But Charlie loved the boys for who they were; he never focused on what he was giving up. He was a great husband and father. He worked hard to support the family, and whenever I needed him, Charlie was there.

We didn't know if the effort was working. The seizures had lessened, but they weren't gone. The boys were susceptible to colds and other minor illnesses, but for them, no illness was minor. Worst of all, we didn't know how they were feeling. I believed they were happy, that they appreciated museums and the zoo, but they couldn't laugh or clap, much less talk. Marshall has poor vision, and I wasn't sure what he could see. Coulton would rock back and forth, unfocused and making unintelligible noises. Were they in pain? Were they happy? Were they fulfilled? Did they love me? Was there anything more I could do?

The Christmas Marshall was three and a half, we gave him a toy with five large buttons featuring pictures of animals. When you pushed a button, it would make the appropriate animal noise. I held Marshall on my lap, and we played with that toy. Marshall couldn't reach for the buttons, but he could hear the sounds each animal made.

"Cat," I'd say, and the toy would meow, and Marshall would relax.

"Lion," I'd say, and the toy would roar, and Marshall would rock forward, almost as if he was signaling, *Yes, more.*

We played with that toy every day for weeks, because I knew it made Marshall happy. I'd hold him on my lap, close to my chest, and I could feel his excitement.

"Dog." *Bark.* Marshall would lean forward.

"Bird." *Tweet tweet.* I could feel the thrum in his chest.

"Cat," I said one day, and Marshall rocked forward, excited, and touched a button with his forehead. *Meow.*

I stopped. Did he just push the cat button?

"Marshall," I said, "could you push the cat button again?"

He leaned forward. He bent his forehead to the toy. *Meow.*

I was stunned. Maybe it was an accident? "Marshall," I said, "which button is the lion?"

He leaned his head and touched a button. *Roar.*

I asked about the dog. He touched the dog. I asked about the lion. He touched the lion. I stopped. I couldn't speak, I was so overwhelmed. Marshall knew the buttons. He had been watching and listening. All those days, as I played with him, he had been learning. He knew what was happening in the world around him and why. Maybe he had always known. He just hadn't known how to tell me.

CHAPTER 4

PLANTING SEEDS

Years ago I read an article that has stuck with me ever since. It said the people who are lucky are the people who make connections. I love that idea, because it builds on something I've always believed: that successful people find the best experts and ask for their assistance.

I had always leaned on Dad. After my marriage, I leaned on Charlie. But I'd leaned on others, too. The owner of the Pontiac dealership had taught me about cars. The professors at Vanderbilt had stayed after class to answer my endless questions. The workers at the sand mine had appreciated my willingness to consult them, and the experts at the Environmental Health Center had given me a blueprint for a healthier life for my boys.

So I knew if I was going to reach Marshall—really reach him—I needed help. Fortunately, I had a resource right down the road: the University of Texas. After a good bit of research (and some lucky connections), I was introduced to Dr. Keith Turner, a professor of education. Professor Turner was a big burly man with dimples, a gentle giant with a genuine love of children with special needs. It was a perfect match. He needed research subjects for a project on new teaching methods. I needed someone who could show me how to support my son.

After some introductory testing for compatibility, Dr. Turner came to our house with a video camera. He set up the camera to film Marshall, who was on my lap, then folded his long body behind the table across from us.

"Marshall," he said. "Why don't we play a game?"

He pulled out an oversized picture book and opened it to a page with two animals. "Show me the lion."

Marshall slowly tilted his head until he touched the right picture.

Keith flipped to a new page. "Let's try a harder one. Can you touch the striped animal?"

Marshall bent his head to touch the zebra.

"Very good," Keith said, and Marshall tapped his heels together. That was Marshall's way, I knew, of showing he was happy. The faster he tapped, the happier he was.

He tapped whenever I told him Professor Turner was coming to film him, and he tapped when, between their sessions, I shared books with him. At first, I focused on the pictures, but soon I realized that Marshall liked it when I read longer passages. I bought him some headphones, so that when I was taking care of Coulton, he could listen to music or books on tape. I was amazed by how calm he became. Marshall was only four, but he could focus on music or an audiobook for an hour or more.

I remember the first time Keith said, "Let's try something difficult, Marshall." He turned to a page with two words on it:

"giraffe" and "lion." "One of these words says 'lion.' Can you tell me which one?"

No way, I thought. But Marshall didn't hesitate. He bent his head and touched the word "lion." He could read.

I created an alphabet board. It was white poster board on a stiff back, with two-and-a-half-inch-tall dark blue letters. I added a few shortcuts, such as the word "Marshall," but for the most part, Marshall would have to "type" his thoughts one letter at a time. I knew he could identify words. I'd watched him do it for months. But this was different. Could Marshall communicate?

I placed him on my lap. I'm sure he could feel my excitement as I lifted the board and explained to him the possibilities. It took months for him to control his movements, but eventually, Marshall learned how to reach out and tap letters with the knuckle of his curled hand. I had doubted that he would ever be able to communicate complex thoughts. I had hoped, if anything, he could tell me his immediate needs. Hungry. Sad. Foot hurts. Over the next months, I watched in astonishment as Marshall began to create different kinds of messages:

Listen to God's thoughts, he wrote for Easter.

Good finds the sweet giver.

Marshall never expressed any sadness. He never considered trivial things, and why would he, when it often took an hour to write a sentence, touching each letter laboriously with his fist? He wrote instead, over and over again, of three things: goodness, God, and love.

That fall, when Marshall was five and a half, Charlie and I attended a charity event featuring artwork drawn by an autistic child. We bought a drawing of horses for Marshall, because we're from Texas, and people from Texas love horses. We also met the sponsor of the auction, Dr. Laurence Becker, an educator who worked with autistic children. When he heard our story, he wanted to meet Marshall. A few weeks later, he watched with fascination as Marshall spelled out messages with his board.

"Keep everything he writes," Dr. Becker told me.

And since that day, I have.

For the most part, Marshall wrote letters. He wrote short messages to Charlie and me. He became pen pals with Ryerson Johnson, a nonagenarian who had written dozens of books beginning in the 1940s, mostly Westerns. "We must be the oldest writer and youngest writer in America," Ryerson wrote in one of their first exchanges.

His most frequent correspondent, though, was my dad. Charlie and I had always believed in and cherished our sons, but right behind us, every step of the way, was my father. He had accepted the boys exactly as they were—perfect souls with imperfect bodies—from the moment they were born. He had helped me see them that way, too. He had never questioned the decisions Charlie and I made, and he never thought we were foolish for talking to the boys as if they could understand us.

Even a towering oak, with time, must bend. That's the nature of life. Dad bent toward Marshall. He had always stood above me, but with my son, Dad came down. He sat with Marshall. He held him. Once Marshall started writing, he and Dad began to exchange letters. I mean the old-fashioned kind, written by hand (in Dad's case) and mailed in an envelope with a stamp. Marshall was so excited when he received a letter from Dad. He tapped his heels together when I showed him the envelope, and he tapped as I read it to him, and often he started nodding, which meant he wanted his board. There was a beautiful simplicity in what they wrote to each other. The letters were about love, and they were filled with love. Often they were one sentence, but always, that was enough.

I remember Dad playing dominos one evening with Marshall. These were enormous, colorful cardboard dominos, so that Marshall could easily point with his head to the play he wanted. Marshall was only five, but he was winning every game, and after a while Dad turned to me and said, "Who's to say Marshall isn't the perfect one, Troy, and we aren't the ones who need to learn?"

For Christmas that year, I ordered Dad personalized stationery and envelopes, because nothing was more important to either of us than his letters. When the order arrived, I realized the envelopes didn't include his return address.

"That's all right," Dad said with a smile on Christmas morning. "I don't know where I'll be living anyway."

He kissed Marshall to thank him. He kissed me. Less than a week later, Dad died of an aneurysm. He was only sixty years old.

"I'd still be happy if I died now," he had told Charlie a few days before Christmas, "because I've lived seven lives."

He didn't want to go. I know that. He loved life, and he loved his family. He had a pure heart. But I guess he sensed the end was coming. Dad was the oak, and he had always sheltered us. But this imperfect body, in the end, will betray us all.

CHAPTER 5

LISTENER'S HILL

Raising children can be lonely, especially for mothers like me, who have worked outside the home. Suddenly, your social interactions drop from dozens every day to two or three: your husband, your children, maybe the clerk at the grocery store. Most mothers develop routines: playdates, sports teams, volunteer work, school functions. They make friends with other mothers, because they have similar schedules and experiences.

It doesn't work like that with special needs children. I couldn't take the boys out. I couldn't share my experiences with others in the neighborhood. I had always cherished my large group of female friends, but as the boys grew older, they began to drift away. They didn't know how to react when Coulton screamed. They didn't know how to talk to Marshall. They wanted to talk about their children, who were walking, reading, getting good grades, but after a few sentences, they'd fall silent, embarrassed. Were they cruel to mention their successes? Were they selfish? Was it okay, they wondered, that they *pitied* us?

After five years with the boys, my circle was so small, I could count my friends on one hand. Rosie, my best friend from college, who lived in Alabama but visited often. Aan, whom I had tried to comfort when she lost her ten-day-old son and who always made time for me. Charlie. My sister Trish. My mother, who had come back to me. Mom was a giver; she lived to take care of us. Mom was the only other person Marshall wrote with at his alphabet board, and she was the only person, besides Charlie, I trusted to watch the boys while I went to the store or took a shower. She cooked for us. Mom was a great cook. She cleaned. She was there for me, even if she still didn't approve of my medical choices. I could see it in the way she shook her head or turned away from me, and that's a hard thing, to live with your mother's disapproval.

And then I lost Dad.

I still remember the phone call. The air rushed out of me, not just because the man I had loved so dearly and for so long was gone, but because it was so unexpected. I turned around, and it was so strange that the room looked the same, that the clouds were still in the sky outside. How could everything just keep going?

I was lost. I was depressed and unsure. Dad had been intense and demanding, but he had loved me without judgment, and he had been wise. I thought of all the times he had supported me with his faith over the years and all the good advice he had given me. *Learn to sell. If you can sell, you'll never go hungry. No just means they don't have enough information yet. You know what to do, now I want to hear that you've done it.*

How could so much be gone so soon?

Eventually, the pain became so intense that I wrote Dad a

letter. I put in everything I wanted to say to him and all the wisdom he'd given me. Then I stashed the letter away. A few weeks later, I took the letter to the ranch he had built with my mother. The property had been sold, but I scaled the fence and walked deep into the large pine forest Dad had planted when he was riding high. I found a shady spot and got down on my knees. It was quiet, so I know Dad heard me when I read him that letter and said good-bye. Then I dug a hole, buried my heart, and walked back to my life.

I was lucky. I know that. And not just because Marshall could communicate his love, or because I still had my mother, or because being so busy with the boys kept my loneliness and loss at bay. I was lucky, primarily, because Charlie and I were doing well financially. Raising special needs children is expensive. It can easily run twenty thousand dollars a year per child. That burden, on top of the loss of a loved one, can crush many families.

Fortunately, a few months before Marshall was born, Charlie's grandfather had given us $10,000. Dad never gave me money; that wasn't his style. He taught me to be an entrepreneur instead. So Charlie and I used his grandfather's gift for a down payment on a $100,000 piece of undeveloped land in Austin.

"Divide it into large lots," Dad advised us, "and pre-sell them right away. That will give you income to close the sale. Then use the rest of the proceeds as a down payment on another piece of property."

I listened to Dad. Soon, Charlie and I had grown that one piece of land to three, and then six, without spending an extra dime out of our pockets.

"You have to leverage," Dad told us. "It's the only way to turn something small into something big." "Leverage" means that you buy something large on credit, with a small up-front payment. Then you borrow against the value of the large holding to purchase something else, and keep rolling those loans and sales of old assets into more and bigger things. I wouldn't recommend it for everyone. Leveraging is a risky way to live, because your debt can be a hundred times your income. But leverage was Dad's way, so it was mine, too. And if you're good at property management, and you live in an up-and-coming place like Austin, Texas, in the 1990s, you can succeed beyond your dreams.

In the beginning, Charlie and I were partners. We would find properties together, walk the land, come up with a plan. Charlie would handle the engineering, like roads and utilities, and I would handle the marketing. I even got a real estate license so I could help with the buying and selling of the lots. Our property business wasn't a full-time job—Charlie was still working full-time as a project manager for a national real estate company—but it was profitable and fulfilling.

Then Marshall and Coulton became my priority, and they began to take up more and more of my time. By the time Marshall was five—the year Dad died—I was deeply embroiled in proving to the local school that my son could learn. Public schools often don't want to take the time to nurture kids like Marshall because they cost too much. They want to stick them in a room and forget them, or, more conveniently, shove them out of the system. Often the school systems succeed. It's tough to fight the state, in addition to everything else.

I had an advantage: I had enough money and stamina to challenge them, and I had Marshall's alphabet board. I could fight for Marshall's rights and, hopefully, create opportunities for similar children. But that meant walking away from our real estate ventures.

Then Charlie began developing our properties, working as his own contractor and manager. That increased our revenue, but it was a double hit for me: Charlie now had less time with the family, and he needed me less. I kept a hand in design and layout decisions, but Charlie handled the daily details. Eventually, he quit his corporate job and founded a development company. I was a partner in the business, and I still offered advice (because I always offer advice), but Charlie was taking control of our partnership, and I know, looking back, that losing my business role contributed to the deep sense of loss that settled over me in the years following Dad's death.

So in 1994, exactly twenty years after Dad bought his ranch, we leveraged our investments to buy a derelict farm seventeen miles west of Austin and moved my family to the country. The distance to the hospital was a problem, since one of the boys was sick almost every week, but the trade-off was worth it, because the ranch was my project. I didn't have to feel guilty about doing something for myself, because I was going to create a paradise for the boys.

For the next seven years, Charlie and I invested most of our extra income into Listener's Hill, as Marshall named the property. We fixed up the ranch house first, installing wide doors and special bathrooms to accommodate the boys. We built a mile-long walking trail around the property, so that I could push them in their wheelchairs. Dad had loved trees; he had planted almost four thousand on his once dusty, treeless ranch. I planted trees on Listener's Hill so that the boys could hear the breeze. Marshall asked for a quiet space of his own, so we transformed a derelict stone building into a peaceful retreat. We painted it white inside and put in prints by old masters, a porch swing, and a small bed with safety rails, so that Marshall could lie alone and listen to classical music or books on tape. Marshall loved it. He named it the Thoughtful House.

What wonderful concepts. A house to be thoughtful in. A hill to listen from. That was Marshall. Listening. Thinking. That was his whole world.

But Listener's Hill wasn't just for the boys, as I realized years later. I couldn't find a way to interact with adults in Austin, so subconsciously, I built a place that would draw them to me. The first to come was Mom, who moved into a small outbuilding behind the main house. My sister Trish, a single mother with two children, moved into a larger outbuilding. A physical therapist named Gerald worked with the boys in their school therapy program (Mom also volunteered). He was so good with them that, at the end of the year, I invited him to live in another little house at Listener's Hill rent free, and he did for several years. The property development business was thriving, especially after Charlie wrangled the most sought-after private commission in Austin: the construction contract for the home of Michael Dell, the founder of the Dell computer company. I plunged some of those profits into building a horse barn at Listener's Hill, because I love horses and they are great therapy for children with special needs.

At its heart, this story is about entrepreneurship. I think. Or it's about pursuing your dreams . . . Or maybe it's about family, and love, and the joy you find in both.

Fortunately, I don't have to know what this story is about. The meaning is whatever touches your heart. For me, all those things—entrepreneurship, family, a community of love—have been bound up with horses.

I was fourteen when Dad moved our family to the ranch. There was a tidy little horse barn on the property, and the more I looked at it, the more I wanted a horse. Dad said no, no, no, but I got a bunch of Thoroughbred auction catalogs and marked my favorites. This was at the height of Dad's fortune. He was driving the Lincoln and wearing yellow diamonds. Why couldn't his loyal child benefit, too?

"You really want this, don't you?" Dad said finally, eyeing me carefully as I handed him the catalogs for the twentieth time. You never get anything in life, after all, by giving up. No just means they don't yet have the information they need to say yes.

"Yes, Dad. And I've marked some good ones that won't be too expensive. You'll see."

He flipped through the pages. "Are you willing to work for this?"

"Yes, Dad."

"Then let's go."

We went to the auction, and Dad bought eleven horses. Eleven! I only wanted one. A good one. Dad bought the worst eleven horses at the sale: the ones that were only a few hundred dollars, because they stank, and nobody else wanted them.

"They're your responsibility now," Dad said of his investment. "I expect you to groom them, train them, feed them, clean the stables, whatever else horses require."

He had no idea how much work it was. I was a freshman in high school and I had a job selling advertising for Dad's radio station. Now I was waking up at five in the morning and spending twenty or more hours every week caring for horses.

"What are you thinking about doing with them?" Dad asked a few months later, when we were sitting together on the porch one night.

"I found one I like," I told him. He smiled. He knew that would happen. "I thought maybe I could show him."

Dad thought for a minute. "Do you have to pay to enter these competitions?"

"Yes, sir."

"Well, what if you held a competition here and charged people to enter it, instead of paying for someone else's show? What would you need for that?"

"I'd need a riding ring. A hunt field. Seats for spectators. I'd need trophies."

Dad nodded. "I wonder how you'd pay for all that," he muttered. That's how he worked. He would throw out an idea—planting seeds, he called it—and I'd sink my teeth into it and never let it go.

A few weeks later, Dad asked how the project was going.

"I've checked with advertisers," I said. "They're interested. But I don't think the money will be enough to build a ring and a hunt field."

Dad nodded. He thought for a while. "What if you made it a series of competitions?" he said. "Say five, with points accumulated each round so they'd have to come back for each one. It wouldn't cost much more, but you could sell a lot more advertising."

And that's how I ended up running my first profitable business: a quarterly horse show on our ranch. I oversaw the building of the facilities, sold the advertising, created the brochures, hired the judges, sold merchandise, and managed it all. It took hundreds of hours of work, and a lot of organizing and persuading, but with the help of my friends and siblings, I got everything done. I was fifteen.

I ran the Run of Champions for two years, but I had to give up the horses when I went to college. So the horse barn at Listener's Hill wasn't just for the boys, it was also for me. I knew I could support the stables, and a few good horses, if I turned it into a business. Instead of starting a competition, I partnered with a trainer named Carol, who was recently divorced and needed something new in her life. She moved to Listener's Hill, and we started horseback riding classes for children and a therapy riding program. I don't know what it is about horses, but they can have an extraordinary effect on the young, especially kids with special needs. Even Coulton, whose joys were so narrow, was happy on horseback, and more importantly, he was calm. Horses can touch children's souls.

Marshall fell in love with a big palomino and named it Goldie. Goldie was his horse; he'd ride her as often as we could lift him onto her high back. But other children rode Goldie as well, and there was a girl who loved Goldie, too. The horse made such a positive change in her life, and in her mother's life, that when they left, I sold her to them. Marshall agreed to it, but he was still crushed to lose his friend. He rode other horses for two years, until he found a new horse he loved almost as much as Goldie. I told him this time the horse could be his, and his alone.

He clicked his heels, he was so happy. He named the horse . . . Justice.

CHAPTER 6

TWO GIFTS

The last and most important addition to our extended family at Listener's Hill arrived in 1993, when Charlie and I were given the opportunity to adopt another child. We had wanted more children of our own, but with our genetic predisposition, we couldn't take the risk. The adoption agencies disqualified us, because we were already caring for Marshall and Coulton. Another child seemed beyond our reach, but we had the luck of connections. A church friend knew a young woman who was pregnant. A family was going to adopt her baby, but the biological father wouldn't give up his rights, and the adopting parents backed out. They didn't want to take the chance that, in a year or two, they'd lose the child they had come to love.

I asked Marshall what he thought. "Mama needs a good baby," he wrote.

That phrase . . . those two words. Marshall could break my heart.

I spoke to the mother of the pregnant girl. Her daughter was desperate to keep her child out of the foster care system, she said. If we were willing to take him straight from the hospital, without guarantees, she would agree to the adoption.

I said we'd take him. We already loved him. "When is he due?"

"Next week," the mother said.

We named him Luke. That was Marshall. I wanted to name him Logan or Ryan, but when I suggested those names my seven-year-old wrote back, "Luke already has a name."

He wrote his new brother a poem, entitled "Love to Luke":

> Mercy should know our love for that sweet James Luke.
> Listen to my pure, clear, happy,
> Free brother emerge, feeling joyous.
> I know I might dream of knowledge like sweetness
> That Good shows to us in that dear fine Luke.

Luke was not a good baby, as Marshall had predicted. He was an *exceptional* baby. He was strong and ruddy, with striking red hair, even as an infant. I held him in my arms every day and stared at him, wondering at his tiny hands and quiet eyes. I loved him as I had loved Marshall and Coulton, as if he was my own. Because he *was* my own. I had chosen him. Or more exactly, God had chosen him for me. If my journey to Listener's Hill had been a quest for family, Luke was the culmination.

Those weren't easy days. Anyone who has raised three boys—never mind two with special needs—will know how true that is. I was sleep deprived and run off my feet for years. I was nailed to Listener's Hill, barely able to leave for a quick errand. But this was the world I had created, once the life I had imagined for myself was gone. This was my sanctuary. I could ride with Marshall and Coulton—Luke never liked horses, even when he was older, much to my regret. I could watch Luke walk across his room, then run freely across the lawn, then climb the small trees I had planted when we first arrived on the property, which were growing up alongside him.

I could watch Charlie teach Luke to catch, while I sat with my other boys in the shade, and I could say, "I love you, Luke," and make him squirm and stick out his tongue.

There were downsides to Listener's Hill. We were isolated. The schools and hospitals were far away. Marshall and Coulton had always been sickly. In fact, the doctors had told me they wouldn't live into their teens, and the environment in the Texas Hill Country wasn't helping. Because of the area's location and topography, there is an intense concentration of allergens, and the weather patterns cause them to accumulate in and around Austin. Marshall and Coulton struggled with allergies at Listener's Hill, which would often turn into pneumonia.

But that wasn't much different from our lives in Austin. For years, I had spent sixteen hours a day mothering my boys, helping them communicate and expanding their horizons, but I had monitored their health twenty-four hours a day, seven days a week. I was always on alert for signs of distress, always praying I would act before anything bad happened. Long before Listener's Hill, I had bought equipment to monitor their lung capacity and oxygen intake, and breathing masks and oxygen tanks for emergencies. Many times, that equipment saved their lives. It is not a stretch to say that, for the seventeen years Marshall and Coulton lived in Texas, my life was dedicated to keeping them alive, and many, many times, I almost failed.

On several occasions, Charlie and I even discussed leaving

for a better climate. But we didn't know if that would make a difference, given the boys' other serious health problems, and Marshall loved Listener's Hill, and so did I. It was the only home Luke had known. It was the only happiness I had found.

Marshall never worried. Not about his health, what people thought of him, or what he was missing. He didn't focus on the material world of muscles and bones. He wrote often at Listener's Hill using his alphabet board, but never with bitterness or despair. He believed in good thoughts, kind words, and his ability to teach, if he was given a chance. As he described himself:

> I see myself as a teacher that knows about God.
> Good thoughts come to me and they teach.

In 1996, when he was ten and a half and Luke was a rambunctious three, Marshall told me he wanted to write Charlie a book for Christmas. It was October. Marshall wrote slowly. It wasn't his mind. He always seemed to know exactly what he wanted to say. It was translating his thoughts to a language, through his alphabet board, that the rest of us could understand. Writing a book by Christmas was out of the question.

I had taken Dr. Becker's advice to record and keep everything Marshall wrote, though, so I had six years of material. "Why don't you compile your favorite pieces," I suggested, "and give that to your father?"

Marshall agreed. He and I spent hours together in his Thoughtful House, going over his writings. I would read to him while he lay on his safety bed, staring at the ceiling. It was one of the most peaceful times of my life, as I dove deeper than ever before into the wisdom of my silent son. Occasionally, Marshall would indicate a favorite by tapping the word "yes"

on his alphabet board. Otherwise, the world seemed like nothing more than the spinning of his ceiling fan and his careful
words dropping into the special places between us.

I had always known Marshall's writing was special. I mean,
my child wrote this when he was six, in a piece entitled "My
Harmony Prevails to Free":

> Even though my individuality finds sweet knowing perfec-
> tion I listen for the answers to wishes from above. I listen
> to good thoughts like something over mountaintops. Fine
> messages clearly govern my thinking. Feelings grow har-
> moniously, making love possible.

Eventually, he asked me (through his alphabet board) to
buy him a Bach album. I had played classical music for Marshall and Coulton, but I didn't realize he knew Bach, much less
that he especially liked his music. After listening to the album I
bought him, Marshall wrote this:

> The wind changes direction.
> There is lovely music that feels soft.
> Marshall is there thinking
> lornfully gorgeous thoughts.
> I, listening marvelously
> juxtaposed in wonderment
> finding solitude near!

He called it "Remember Rooms Rest."

Where did he learn such language? How could he know
these words? "Lornfully," I discovered later, was a word he
made up. He learned the others, I suspect, by listening to
books on tape. Marshall preferred classics, so his phrases were

often old-fashioned and occasionally antique. He once wrote
the word "brough." I told him that this wasn't a word, but he
insisted. I looked it up in the dictionary. It wasn't there. Marshall insisted. I finally found it in an unabridged dictionary. It
is an archaic word that means "a ring or halo." That's exactly
the way Marshall had used it:

> irreverently, marvelously, nearing the brough of Good God.

Despite his sophisticated language, it was the simplicity of
Marshall's message that moved my heart, once I sat with him
in the Thoughtful House and read everything straight through.
Marshall's writings were beautiful variations on the similar
themes. They revolved around the ideas of listening, feeling,
loving, teaching, and respecting everyone and everything. He
wrote often of God, beginning with a piece he called "Altogether Lovely."

> God is good and merciful
> because He is also bright and intelligent.
> Seeing, feeling all that is true.
> Clearly He feels and listens to all our desires.
> Clearly He has everybody's
> dreams in mind.
> I see a God altogether lovely.

And he wrote often of teaching others to find peace:

> I have a dream of careful definition
> bearing good love
> definitely greatly balanced with harmony,
> caring how real people feel.

When his favorite one hundred pieces were taken together—some only a few words, some full poems or letters—there was a peacefulness and tranquility I had never expected to find. It was the peace I felt on all those afternoons with Marshall, in his stone house on Listener's Hill.

"Nicely think of being a good Dad," Marshall wrote to Charlie when we gave him his Christmas gift. "Know that I feel nice, for each day good Marshall realizes he gently has a perfect Dad."

I had made a hundred copies of the book. This was before print on demand, so that was the minimum I could order. I gave several of those copies to family and friends. I also gave one to Dr. Becker, who had stayed in touch with Marshall over the years and who was, in addition to being an educator, an advocate for children with special needs. His suggestion, after all, had made the compilation possible.

Dr. Becker called me a few weeks later. He wanted to know if I had more copies he could share with friends and colleagues.

A few weeks after that, he called to say a library was interested in a public reading. "People love the book," he said, "and they love Marshall. You can read his words, and he can be there."

We printed five hundred copies of Kiss of God and donated them to the library, but in the end, Charlie and I went without Marshall, who was ill with a respiratory infection. The reading was in Dripping Springs, Texas. To my surprise, the library was packed. Luck is created by connections, right? Dr. Becker must have known the right people.

The librarians asked us to come back a few weeks later. The second reading had even more people than the first, but Marshall's health was still fragile, and he didn't attend.

"Where's Marshall?" everyone asked. "We want to meet Marshall."

For the third reading, we brought Marshall. He was clicking his heels, excited, as we wheeled him in front of the audience. I read from his writings and a special note he had composed for that night. At the end, people stood to applaud. Many, like me, were wiping tears from their eyes.

"Marshall gives thoughts to more people," Marshall wrote when I asked him what he thought of the book.

How could I say no? I had been told Marshall would never do anything with his life. He would never develop. He would never learn. I would never know my own son. The doctors were wrong. But even with his alphabet board, Marshall lived in a small world. He couldn't travel or talk. He couldn't walk or hold a book. He wrote to family and a few friends, because they were the only people who knew him. His world consisted almost entirely of Listener's Hill and our community there.

Marshall wanted to be a teacher. Please understand that I never thought Marshall would *want* anything. So if he wanted to "give thoughts to more people," and the door was open for me to try, I was going to do it. Like most mothers, I would run to hell and back, if I had to, to make my son's wishes come true.

The trip turned out to be much shorter than to hell. Luck is the result of connections, I saw once again. Our lucky connections went from Dr. Becker, to the Dripping Springs library, to the local Barnes & Noble, to Peter Vegso, the publisher of *Chicken Soup for the Soul,* who agreed to publish Marshall's writings. When good people help with a pure heart, anything is possible.

But you have to work, too, and since Marshall wasn't physically capable, I threw myself into the job. At the publisher's request, I wrote about when and why Marshall had written his pieces (I had recorded that information, too) and convinced

Dr. Becker to write a foreword. I made a short video of Marshall at his board, so readers would understand how he wrote and what his life was like. I made flyers and posters, talked to anyone who would listen, and worked with a twenty-two-year-old Austin-based publicist.

"We're going to get Marshall on *Oprah*," she said.

Whoa, I thought. You know everything isn't *actually* possible, right, no matter how noble your intention and how hard you work?

Apparently Oprah was possible, because Marshall appeared on her show about child prodigies in 1999. She read selections from his book *Kiss of God*. The next week, the book appeared on the *New York Times* bestseller list and Marshall, back home at Listener's Hill with another respiratory infection, began to receive letters from admirers around the world, a wish he had expressed in his own special way in the book's dedication.

> I hope to gather thinkers,
> to give them my thoughts about Love.
> Love to clean their ideas.
> That cleaning might loosen the love
> in their hearts.
> Good thinkers take LOVE to heart
> like gold in the evening, wild sun.

It had been a long climb: eleven years since Marshall pushed that button on his animal toy. Over that time, I had built a relationship with my son, letter by letter, and a home for my family on Listener's Hill. I had supported a business with my horses that offered love and comfort to vulnerable children, even if it didn't make much money. I had expanded my family with

Luke, who filled it with even more love. I had carved a fulfilling life for myself out of what God had given me, and most importantly, I had helped Marshall carve a fulfilling life out of what God had given him.

But nothing gold can stay, as Robert Frost once wrote, even Marshall's wild evening sun.

CHAPTER 7

THE END

It was autumn 2003, late in the afternoon. Marshall was in his bedroom, recovering from another bout of pneumonia. I was in the living room talking with Charlie and my friend Carol, my partner in the horses, when I had a premonition. This happens with mothers, especially those who have been caring for a very sick child for seventeen years. Maybe my mind noticed a deeper quiet. Maybe something beeped, or I heard under the conversation a strangled breath or a cry. Whatever it was, I knew Marshall needed me.

I went to his room. He was having trouble breathing. His numbers were low when I tested him on the oxygen monitor, but that was common. I had dealt with it a hundred times in the last seven or eight years. This felt different, and I knew by then to trust my instincts.

I called an ambulance.

It didn't feel like enough. I didn't want to wait. I turned to

Charlie, who had been alerted by my concerns. "We need to take Marshall to the hospital right now," I said.

He didn't question me. He picked up Marshall and carried him to the car. We met the ambulance on the road two miles from our house. Marshall and Charlie transferred into the ambulance, while I followed in the car, relieved the professionals were now in charge. But when I got to the hospital, Charlie was agitated and pacing the emergency room.

"What's wrong?" I asked.

He didn't answer. I grabbed his arm. "What's wrong, Charlie?"

"Marshall stopped breathing in the ambulance," he said. "The suction pump wasn't working. The EMTs didn't know what to do."

Marshall had flatlined. Charlie had reached into his mouth to clear his throat, while the paramedics tried to restart his heart. They got it pumping. Barely. Unevenly. Now Marshall was fighting for his life in the emergency room, and Charlie was in shock. Our son had almost died, right in front of his eyes.

That's it, I thought through the tears. *That's all I can take. I can't do this anymore.*

It was fall. Allergy season in Austin. The boys were always sick in the fall. For years, I had considered it a burden. That day in the hospital, I realized it was worse. Living in Texas was going to kill my sons.

"When Marshall gets well," I told Charlie, because I was his mother, and I knew Marshall would survive, because he had to, "we are moving away."

Charlie and I had spent our whole lives in Texas. We had lived in Austin for two decades. We loved it on Listener's Hill. Loved it. But Charlie didn't argue. We knew what we had to do, and I could hear Dad's words, echoing in my heart: *I want to hear you've done it. Not later. Now.*

Marshall recovered. It took weeks, but our son came home. Six months later, we sold Listener's Hill, packed up the life I'd spent forty-four years building, and left Texas forever.

PART II

Angelwood

ANSWERS COME WHEN WE ARE

IN OUR RIGHT PLACE.

CHAPTER 8

ASHEVILLE

Asheville, North Carolina, sits almost half a mile up in the Blue Ridge section of the Appalachian Mountains, amid some of the most gorgeous natural beauty in the United States. The Appalachians don't have the towering, craggy peaks of the Rockies; they are an older mountain chain, worn down over hundreds of millions of years into gentle curves. The peaks recede like thoughts, the front ridges crisp and blue, the back ridges fading into the clouds that give the nearby Great Smoky Mountains their name until, eight or nine ridges away, they finally disappear. It's a quiet beauty. It calms the soul, with its subtle greens and blues, before bursting out, for a month in the fall, in spectacular red, yellow, orange, and gold. And then it fades, slowly, into bare limbs and biting wind, with the promise of spring always on the horizon, like the last ridge in a twenty-mile view.

The first Europeans here were tough mountain people, subsistence farmers who settled on the gentler slopes. They were predominantly Scots-Irish, and they brought with them a self-sufficiency that included a tradition of making whiskey and a hatred of paying taxes on their homemade liquor. In Europe, they had made their whiskey out of barley; in the mountains, they made it out of the grain that grew best on their small mountain farms: corn. They gave it to their friends, sold it alongside their fresh eggs, and kept a bottle in the cabinet, either straight or infused with herbs, to combat minor ailments like toothaches and coughs. Circuit-riding preachers carried it from town to town and even, on occasion, served it at church. The liquor was easier to transport than corn and more valuable, so it became a staple of the local economy, bartered for everything from seeds to cattle to hand-stitched bridal gowns. Appalachia, after all, was isolated country; until the railroad reached Asheville in 1880, the region was largely inaccessible. At the end of the Civil War, the population of Buncombe County, where Asheville is the county seat, was only about twenty-five hundred people, excluding the native Cherokees, who didn't count to the American government and therefore weren't counted.

But the Blue Ridge Mountains had beauty, and with the coming of the railroad, Asheville had a connection to the money and power of the coast. Small factories arrived, mostly textiles and lumber, but more importantly, so did wealthy urbanites escaping the summer heat of Washington, Charleston, Philadelphia, and New York. In the 1880s, Asheville began attracting the Gilded Age aristocracy, and by 1889 the city was wealthy enough to install the first streetcar line in the state of North Carolina. That same year, George Washington Vanderbilt, the grandson of Cornelius Vanderbilt and one of the richest men in America, began building a private summer home on the edge of town. At 178,000 square feet, the Biltmore Estate was and still is the largest private residence in the United States. It had its own train station, a small village to house its workers, and, soon after its completion in 1895, a neighboring community of other wealthy industrialists who wanted access to both Asheville's peaceful beauty and Vanderbilt's vast influence.

Asheville, thriving as never before, went on a modernization spree, establishing courts, building a school system, and bridging the French Broad River, which hemmed in the west side of town. By the 1920s, the downtown was filled with stylishly modern Art Deco buildings, some as tall as ten stories, and the city was the third largest in North Carolina. Resort hotels like the Grove Park Inn, completed in 1913, were attracting tourists and conventions, and both groups were awash in liquor. North Carolina had the largest number of federally licensed stills in the United States, but even Prohibition couldn't stop the Scotch-Irish whiskey that was flowing out of the nearby mountains in rivers. Celebrities like Henry Ford were presented with bottles of pure corn liquor; tourists got drunk on unique local cocktails. One famous cocktail, according to moonshine historian Joseph Earl Dabney, was "twenty-four-hour punch," a drink made by soaking citrus peels in a mixture of corn liquor, sugar, and juice for an entire day. It was deceptively potent. At one convention, guests indulged in so much of the local specialty that no one could get out of bed the next morning. Everybody at that convention, I suspect, couldn't wait for their next trip to Asheville.

Then the Depression hit, and the tourist economy crumbled. Local businesses collapsed, and on one brutal day in November 1930, eight of the nine banks in town failed. The entire Blue Ridge region was devastated, and even twenty-four-hour punch disappeared with the last of the good times. Asheville, a shell-shocked boomtown, was stuck with $56 million in debt (about a billion dollars in today's valuation) and no economic base to generate revenue. Instead of declaring bankruptcy, as many cities did during the Depression, the proud mountain town declared that it would pay back the entire debt. It did. But it took fifty years.

By then, Asheville was a shell of its former self. Essentially broke, the city had let its infrastructure fall into disrepair. The sewer system was outdated; the schools were crumbling; social services were inadequate for the poverty of the region. The population hadn't increased much since the Depression, and half the Art Deco buildings in the downtown business district were vacant and boarded up. After five P.M., when the government offices shut down, there was nobody on the streets. In the late 1970s, the only restaurants downtown were a diner selling biscuits and a Chinese takeout. A highway linked the city to the rest of the South, but Asheville was little more than a brief "Vanderbilt house" stop for tourists on their way to the nearby Blue Ridge Parkway and Great Smoky Mountains National Park.

In the 1980s, large-scale urban renewal projects like South Street Seaport in New York, Underground Atlanta, and Fourth Street Live! in Louisville, Kentucky, began opening across the country. These projects were designed to turn blighted urban downtowns into "entertainment corridors" with restaurants, bars, and pedestrian walkways that would attract tourists and suburbanites. National conglomerates created and managed the projects, and national chains were recruited to fill the retail and dining spaces. One such company proposed demolishing a large section of deserted downtown Asheville and replacing it with an indoor mall. The city government was in favor, but the citizens of Asheville voted it down. This wasn't so much historic preservation. Several proposals to improve the downtown had been made over the decades, and all had failed. The mostly blue-collar citizens of Asheville didn't want to pay higher taxes for a project they didn't believe would succeed. The town motto, as officials joked, was "That won't work here, so don't try." It was mountain wisdom born out of fifty years of failure and stagnation.

But the near destruction of downtown Asheville had another effect: it woke up the area's activist base. Because of its natural beauty and proximity to the famed Black Mountain art collective, Asheville had always attracted writers, musicians, visual artists, environmentalists, hippies, and other free spirits. It also attracted retirees, who were drawn by the cool mountain temperatures and small-town life. These two groups, spearheaded by men like Roger McGuire, a retired executive at *Southern Living,* turned their energy toward saving the historic center of town.

They planned the development of Pack Square Park, a linear lawn near a memorial to Zebulon Vance, a Confederate general and governor. They hired renovation experts to explore uses for the Grove Arcade, a deserted 1920s shopping area originally designed so ladies wouldn't have to walk outside. Roger McGuire rehabilitated a derelict building on Haywood Street into fourteen apartments and four retail spaces, the first conversion of an old commercial space into residences in downtown.

In 1991, Julian Price and a local lawyer, Pat Whalen, founded Public Interest Projects (PIP). Heir to an insurance fortune, Price had moved from California to Asheville, where he had become active in local nonprofits. Looking to focus his efforts, he decided to invest almost all of his inheritance, about $15 million, into rehabilitating downtown. His idea was to

develop residences and encourage people to move in by creating street-level businesses. Public Interest Projects was a for-
profit company with no interest in making a profit. The goal
was to use Price's money to create a vibrant, self-sustaining
community.

The problem was that no banks would loan money for
downtown projects. So PIP offered loans to established local
businesses on very good terms, if they would expand downtown. Laughing Seed, a vegan lunch counter at a suburban
YMCA, became a full restaurant in the heart of the city. Salsa's,
a tiny restaurant with a line perpetually out the door, doubled
its size, then spawned a second downtown restaurant, Zam-
bra. Soon Pat Whalen realized local chefs and artisans were
better at making great products than operating businesses,
so PIP began offering accounting, bookkeeping, and business
development services. They started taking a small interest in
the businesses instead of giving them loans, to lower overhead
costs and make it easier for new entrepreneurs to weather slow
times.

In 1994, PIP opened its first residential development, a
mixed-income apartment complex in a 1918 Art Deco building
they had saved from being razed for a parking lot. The apartments, to everyone's astonishment, were all rented months
before the project was completed.

In 1995, the rumor started that Barnes & Noble was looking to open a downtown Asheville store. PIP approached
Malaprop's, a beloved but small independent bookstore, and
offered them the entire ground floor of their new redevelop-
ment project. The space was raw, filthy, and enormous, so
PIP gave the store a floating rent that would fluctuate with
its sales. Malaprop's asked its loyal customers for assistance
in paying for new shelves and fixtures, and when the commu-

nity responded, the store moved into the larger space. Barnes & Noble scuttled its plans; Malaprop's became famous for its poetry readings and support of local authors. In 2000, *Publishers Weekly* named it "Bookseller of the Year."

By then, Asheville, North Carolina, the little mountain town that couldn't, was being called one of the best small cities in America. By missing out on every development trend since 1929, and by being forced to focus on the passions and talents of the people who lived there and loved it, the city had become the epitome of the urban ideals of the new century. It was compact and walkable, with narrow streets; it was dominated by quirky local businesses; it had numerous pocket parks and grassy squares; and since fifty years of failure meant there had never been a need to build new buildings or tear down old ones, it had a well-preserved historic downtown almost entirely free of blocky, glassy modern architecture and national chains.

Asheville was *happening,* but it wasn't ambitious. It was still the same basic city of artists and blue-collar families, as soft and peaceful as the mountains that surrounded it. People were moving in; they were starting businesses, because Asheville had low overhead costs and an entrepreneurial vibe; but they weren't chasing fortunes. They were chasing happiness, and finding it in the natural beauty, the slower pace, and the artisan style. The 1920s-era bridge across the French Broad, long an afterthought, was crowded with young people settling in cheap, hip West Asheville. The beer-brewing scene was booming, led by Highland Brewing Company, the only craft brewer in Western North Carolina when it opened in 1994. The chef-driven, unpretentious food scene was being touted in the *New York Times* and celebrated in Europe. The tourists who came for the Biltmore Estate were no longer leaving, but staying to experience a downtown filled with refurbished parks, narrow streets, classic architecture, and outdoor dining with a view of the mountains. Just like in the old days, when the conventioneers were drinking twenty-four-hour punch, Asheville was a great place to have a good time.

Julian Price didn't live to see it. He died in 2001, just as Asheville was blossoming. But even then, I think, he knew what his adopted hometown would become. His money had helped fuel a new era. His attitude—from donating dozens of trees to personally fixing broken benches as he walked his beloved downtown streets—had helped sustain it. He never wanted credit or wealth. He had always believed in creating a community, open to and affordable for all. And he had succeeded by cheerfully setting an example and convincing the government, business, and volunteer communities to work together. Men and women like Roger McGuire and Julian Price, in other words, had changed an "it can't happen here" attitude to a belief that Asheville could, with perseverance, a pure heart, and a good plan, be anything it wanted to be.

The ultimate proof of his success, I think, is that most of the people who have moved to or visited Asheville since his death have no idea the city was ever at rock bottom. His organic approach to growth, sustained now for decades, makes Asheville seem like a product of nature, carved into coolness by the same forces that made the mountains, and not a down-on-its-luck town that had been lifted up through brute human effort one inch, one building, and one small business at a time.

CHAPTER 9

WE FIND OUR WAY

We never planned to move to Asheville. When Charlie and I decided to uproot our lives for the boys' health, we had no idea where to go. I didn't want to live in a big city, and I had no intention of leaving the South. So I did a Google search of the best small towns in the region. Then Charlie and I loaded our three sons into our SUV and headed east for a tour.

Fairhope, Alabama. Savannah, Georgia. Charleston, South Carolina. Charlottesville, Virginia.

It was a route I'd followed before, when I was a child. My father had one hobby, besides starting businesses, and that was antiquing. He was not a man of leisure, and he didn't enjoy idle time. Our family vacations, such as they were, consisted of driving around the South in a station wagon with a tow hitch, looking for bargains. I never bothered to think, until years later, how odd it was that even our free time was consumed by my father's passions. It was another wedge, probably, between

Dad and some of my siblings. But never between Dad and me. I remember leaning over the front seat as he drove, asking excitedly about the next stop down the line.

I loved every town Charlie and I visited, and I have fond memories of many. There are places, especially in the South, that don't seem to change. But I was still in mourning over leaving Texas, and none of the cities felt like home. Too small. Too swampy. Too artificial. Too hot. I was done with heat. And I wasn't sure about living close to the ocean. We might have to evacuate for a hurricane or storm. And what about the humidity and salt air? Was that healthy for weak lungs?

Asheville felt different. The afternoon we arrived, Charlie and I pushed the boys all over Biltmore Village, the neighborhood the Vanderbilts had built for their servants and workers, now a charming maze of shops and restaurants with cobblestone streets. We ate at the Corner Kitchen, a local favorite housed in a one-hundred-year-old Victorian mansion, and looked down the long lovely entry drive toward the Biltmore Estate. Someone mentioned the Shindig on the Green, a free bluegrass concert held every few weeks during the summer, so we drove downtown. It only took ten minutes, even with traffic. We walked the narrow streets, marveling at the vibrant businesses. Pack Square Park was filled with lawn chairs and picnickers of all varieties: college kids with piercings and dreadlocks, working families with small children, older people in overalls straight from the mountains. In Austin, people of different ages didn't mix. The main drag, Sixth Street, was wide, hot, and loud, with bars and drunks lining both sides. It was a terrible place to walk two young men in wheelchairs—terrible—and we never felt comfortable there. But here, everyone was welcome. Some nice people even cleared a place for us right in front of the Roger McGuire bandstand, and before long, all three boys were absorbed in the music. The sun settled behind the Art Deco buildings as the bands changed over, then dipped beyond the mountains, turning them golden, then black. Along the edges of the park, people came together with fiddles, banjos, and homemade instruments, playing back and forth in overlapping rhythms and songs.

Charlie and I looked at each other, and we didn't have to say a word. We knew. This was the place. Asheville was where our boys needed to be.

By the end of the week, we'd made an offer on a house in Biltmore Forest that had been a summer getaway for a wealthy industrialist in the 1920s. I wasn't used to having cash. Whatever Charlie and I had made in Texas, we spent. We put it back into new investment properties, or I used it to work on Listener's Hill and buy medical equipment for the boys. In Austin, we were "house poor." Often, we didn't have two spare nickels to rub together, because that was another thing I'd learned from Dad: rubbing two nickels together wasn't worth a dime. Put that money to work.

But once we sold Listener's Hill and our projects in Texas, Charlie and I found ourselves with cash. So we splurged on a dream house. It was more than we needed, but why not? We moved Mom into the house with us, and after a few months, my sister Trish and her kids joined us too. The house had wide halls, a huge fireplace, and a forest out the back window for Luke to play in and the other boys to look at. We had to update the bathroom, including adding an oversized shower to accommodate the boys' bath chairs. We remodeled the bedrooms to make them safe for Marshall and Coulton (and nice for Luke), and Marshall wrote messages to seal inside the walls, including

a favorite phrase that had been painted on his bedroom ceiling
at Listener's Hill:

Understanding takes a dear good listening thinker.

Of course, my routine was much the same in Asheville.
The boys still needed constant care, and it wasn't unusual
for Coulton to shriek or slam drawers for hours. There were
days, I admit, when the constant noise drove me to despair.
But Coulton quiet was always worse. I remember, one afternoon in Austin, being startled to realize the house was silent.
I rushed into the television room to find Luke sitting on a
pillow. Coulton's pencil legs were sticking out, flailing wildly,
but his head and body were covered. Luke, who was three,
didn't mean anything by it. He had gotten frustrated with
Coulton's banging, and he couldn't figure out any other way
to stop him. But it could have ended badly. He could have
killed his brother. Coulton was seven years older than Luke,
but he couldn't defend himself, even from a toddler. He was
completely dependent on me.

But in Asheville, my days felt different. Luke, who was going
into the fifth grade, loved living in a neighborhood for the first
time, and soon he had a circle of nearby friends. Charlie and I
became close with their parents, and through them with others
in the area. Asheville was an older town than Austin, but it was
a town of transplants. Even the successful entrepreneurs had
only been around ten years. This was a place people came for
a fresh start, and many of our neighbors, like us, had picked
up and moved here without jobs or a plan. Asheville had a
vibe that made you feel, no matter what was happening at the
moment, everything would work out okay.

And the weather! It was so pleasant that first summer

that Charlie and I took the boys on long walks almost every day. We'd go to the old downtown Woolworth's department store, which had been converted into an art market with an old-fashioned soda fountain. Across the street was a chocolate store; Malaprop's bookshop was half a block away. Across town was the ten-acre Western North Carolina Farmers Market and, farther out but still only minutes away, the Arboretum, where we could take long walks in the gardens and forests. I couldn't believe how fresh Asheville felt, or how many trees it had. Austin had plenty of trees, but they were mostly juniper, a low and gangly dry-weather variety. In Asheville, the trees were towering and green.

Coulton was a senior in high school, so I spent a lot of time at the end of summer making sure he was taken care of at the public school. I became close with his special education teacher, who suggested I sign him and Marshall up for CAP, a state-run assistance program. I was skeptical. I'd signed up for a similar program in Texas when the boys were little. I waited ten years, but they were never assessed. In fact, I got the call saying they had made it off the waiting list the month we moved to North Carolina. Why put myself through that again, just when I was starting to feel comfortable?

I signed up anyway, fully expecting nothing to happen. Within six weeks, the boys were assessed. Charlie and I met with a counselor, who told us both boys qualified for twelve-hour home health care support. Together, we created a set of monthly goals for the boys to achieve, and we scheduled appointments to discuss their progress. I was stunned. As it turned out, the program was nationwide, but it was jointly funded by the federal government and the state. Apparently, Texas had refused to fund its share, so the program essentially didn't exist there.

That was typical, really, of how I had felt in Texas. The message had always been clear: *We don't care about you or your children. We don't have the money. In fact, we'd rather you go away.*

In Texas, the support came from the schools, so I would have to fight every year for assistance. The teachers and therapists who worked with the boys were wonderful. I will never forget the young teacher's aide who called me to school one day, a thrill in her voice. She had created a rotating platform for Coulton to lie on. Beneath, a circle was divided into four colored areas. I watched in amazement as Coulton, who had never shown any ability to learn, spun on his platform, dropping colored blocks onto the corresponding part of the circle. He was so happy. The teacher and I were in tears. She loved Coulton. She was so proud of him.

But at the end of the year, we lost her. I tried to get her to move to the next grade with Coulton, but the school system wouldn't let her. We had to start over every year, with new people who didn't know or understand the boys. That's the reason I moved Gerald to Listener's Hill. He was so good with the boys, I couldn't stand to lose him.

I have many issues with the North Carolina CAP program. It is contradictory, onerous, and stingy. For poor families, the financial assistance is not enough. The health care workers are trained and managed through Easter Seals, but they are mostly young, inexperienced, and modestly paid. They don't understand how backbreaking and mentally exhausting it is to provide constant care. So turnover is frequent, and my training new caregivers—and more importantly, trusting them—was difficult. I hired a mature Hispanic woman because she told me she'd worked at Panda Express in the mall for sixteen years. I figured if she could do that for so long, she could handle Marshall and Coulton. She's like a family member now. She is the best caregiver the boys have ever had.

What the CAP program really gave me was structure. The boys were in a system, and for all its faults, that was a great comfort. Marshall and Coulton will never be independent. I know that. There is no letting go and no freedom down the road. Charlie and I will never take cruises or drink wine in our empty nest, wondering why our children never call. CAP gave me the assurance I'd have a way to care for them, even if our health or circumstances collapsed.

It felt like . . . freedom. The boys were healthier than they had ever been. I had my support group of Mom, Charlie, Trish, and the CAP professionals. Instead of being separate from the city, as I had been at Listener's Hill, I felt like a part of Asheville, and it was a part of me. The summer was mild, and the fall was spectacular with colors. In December, we took the boys to the Western North Carolina Farmers Market, where there were five enormous open sheds full of Christmas trees. The snow was falling; carolers were singing; Marshall was tapping, Coulton was clapping, and Luke was drinking hot chocolate. It felt exactly like what I wanted Christmas to be.

That spring I bought a map of North Carolina and traced my fingers over the roads. We had rarely traveled for pleasure in Texas; the logistics of wheelchairs, beds, and meals was too difficult, and Coulton hated new things. The idea of driving to another place *for fun* seemed foreign, almost foolish. But one day, as I was tracing the map with Charlie, we stumbled on the town of Marshall, North Carolina, population 872. It was a forty-minute drive northwest of Asheville, along a winding road that followed mountain streams and, eventually, the French Broad River. How could we resist?

We drove out on a Saturday morning in the early summer

of 2005, and the day did not disappoint. Marshall was a lovely little town: a few blocks of redbrick buildings on the far side of a long bridge over the French Broad River. At the end of the bridge sat the domed county courthouse, the tallest building in town. A few shops and restaurants were scattered along Main Street, and a renovated gray clapboard train depot had a sign promising Friday night bluegrass concerts.

It was the mountains, though, that made Marshall special. They rose around the sleepy town, fresh and green, too steep for roads. We took Main Street north along the river. The town disappeared in a few blocks, and the road started to climb. A few miles farther on, we topped a ridge and seemed to leave the modern world behind. On the next ridge, an old farmstead was going to seed, the thigh-high grassy fields dotted with derelict barns. We drove farther, past the occasional house, but this was the deep mountains, and it felt timeless and empty.

Charlie was quiet, but I knew what he was thinking. He hated sitting still. I may have pushed Charlie into our development business, but he'd taken to it like a bear to moonshine mash. (Bears *love* moonshine mash.) He had always worked hard, and he wasn't ready to retire. I had suggested he join a country club or a biking group or something to make contacts and meet friends. Charlie wasn't interested. He didn't drink; he didn't smoke; he didn't play cards. He wanted to be with his family, or he wanted to be working. He really wanted to be doing both.

"Let's do it," I said, thinking that this could be like 1986, the year we bought our first piece of land. It was just Charlie and me then, working side by side.

We bought a piece of property halfway between Asheville and Marshall, about five miles outside the unincorporated crossroads town of Leicester. We planned to develop the back half and keep the front as our vacation property, where a hundred-and-fifty-year-old clapboard house sat in a low area along Sandy Mush Creek, next to the remains of an old tobacco barn and gristmill. The house didn't have a mountain view, but the property was heavily forested, and a creek was better for the boys. Marshall interacted with the world mostly through listening, and the property was alive with the sounds of water and wind. Luke, meanwhile, could turn over rocks looking for crawdaddies and tromp in the shallows, looking for trouble. Marshall named the property Angelwood, a sign of the peace he expected us to find.

I don't think we'd been at Angelwood an hour, though, before a pickup truck pulled into the driveway. An older man got out. He was pushing eighty, a little stiff legged, but with a big smile on his jowly, sun-spotted face. He was wearing a straw Stetson with a feather, a big silver belt buckle, a bolo tie, and ostrich-skin boots.

Oh, brother, I thought, *this guy's a character.*

"I hear you been asking about the neighbors," he said by way of introduction.

That's true. I'd asked around.

"Well, they're good people here," he said, reaching out to shake my hand. "Good people. The only one you got to watch out for is Forrest Jarrett. You best put your wallet in your mouth and tie your shoes on tight when Forrest Jarrett comes around."

"Thanks," I said, shaking his hand. "I'm Troy."

He smiled so broadly that I knew his next words, even before he opened his mouth.

"Pleased to meet you," he said. "I'm Forrest Jarrett."

CHAPTER 10

PET 'N' POKE

Ah, Forrest Jarrett. What would my life be without Forrest Jarrett? I certainly wouldn't be distilling moonshine, that's for sure. And even if I *was* trying, it wouldn't be any good, because I wouldn't appreciate the deep culture of the Appalachian Mountains that created it. Mountain dew, they called the unaged white whiskey that came out of the hollers, before the bright yellow soda came along. Forrest called it white squeezings. Or "brandy; that one's for the ladies," if a canned peach had been put in the jar.

"Let's have a spiderleg," he said when he came around a few weeks later with the first jar of moonshine I'd ever tasted. "Spiderleg" refers to the way the liquor sticks to the side of the glass when you pour in a little dribble.

"Bird can't fly on one wing," he said after finishing, meaning if you've had one spiderleg, you better have two "to level you out."

I didn't join Forrest in the second spiderleg. I wasn't a drinker, especially not of hard liquor, and his moonshine . . . Well, it was terrible. I mean, rotgut, burn-your-esophagus bad.

I didn't say that to Forrest, though. No reason to be rude.

So a few weeks later, he was back with another "pet 'n' poke," as he called his neighborly gifts. It was a tradition he'd learned from his long-gone mother, Mama Linda, who was a master of the pet 'n' poke. She didn't hold with liquor, Forrest said, but she shared everything else. Food. Crafts. Clothing. Gossip. During the big snowstorm of 1935, when the school bus ran off the road at the bend below their two-room cabin, she'd fed thirty-five children out of her own smokehouse and, after the rescue truck ran into the ditch too, put them all up for the night.

Forrest was carrying on the family tradition. He always seemed to know when we were at Angelwood, and he'd never show up empty-handed. He'd have fresh corn from local farmers, apples grown by a friend, or a packet of fresh pork sausage. Mama Linda had made her own sausage, but Forrest cheated, as he said. He had his own proprietary spice blend at a small meatpacker in the area.

And he'd buy in bulk. That was the thing about Forrest: he never wasted a trip. When he brought us a few ears of fresh corn, he'd have a tarp on the back of his truck and corn piled six feet high. When he was giving out pork sausage packs, he was hauling a hundred. Forrest was retired, and he spent his time driving Western North Carolina, giving out pet 'n' pokes and gossiping with his wide network of friends. And when I say "wide," I mean wide. Forrest Jarrett was mountain royalty. He was the Earl of Leicester, as an article in a local magazine, *Capital at Play,* once called him.

When I asked him about the article, Forrest smiled. He had

a sly smile, and it always appeared when he was winding up for a story.

Someone's son had run into trouble. The editor of the magazine, maybe, or an investor, I can't remember. "It was just some high school foolishness, nothing serious, but they were facing some serious consequences," Forrest said, his jowls shaking above his wide shirt collar and bolo tie. "I talked to a few people, and I managed to get those boys a fair deal. A very fair deal." Wink. "Next thing I know, I hear from a writer about an article."

Just another form of a pet 'n' poke, I guess. Forrest was tickled by the article (he kept a stack of the magazines in his truck), except for being quoted saying that "running a railroad out of Roanoke is like trying to have sex standing up in a hammock."

"I told that boy not to print it," he said, tipping back his yellow Stetson. Then he smiled. "I guess it's my fault for saying it."

Forrest. God almighty. He'd been born four miles away, halfway up the mountain above the tiny hamlet of Rector's Corner in the two-room cabin where his great-grandmother Polly O'Dell had been born in 1844. His father had been a small farmer: cattle, corn, and fifteen acres of burley tobacco, "the biggest field this side of the river." Mama Linda had been a talker and good-natured rabble-rouser, like her son. His siblings were Gus T. Blonde and Jewelly Jane, and his ancestors, he liked to say, had come from over off the Low Hole Road.

We struck up a friendship, obviously, and Forrest filled us in on Angelwood. The house had been a stop on the old stagecoach route from Asheville to Hot Springs, and you could still see parts of the overgrown track on the other side of the creek. The shed by the entrance was the pack house, where farmers put the dried tobacco for bundling and pickup, and beside it was the springhouse, a "good place for kissing," Forrest said, because it was designed to keep things cool. Forrest's mother had caught him kissing an older woman in that springhouse once, he said with a smile, and whipped him all the way home.

"You know anyone who could do work on the property?" I asked him.

"Thinkin' about fixing up that barn?" Forrest said, nodding toward the tobacco barn, which was on a rise five or six feet above Sandy Mush Creek. "Would be a nice place to hold a gathering. I got a political thing coming up."

Nothing on the property was usable when we bought it, but according to Forrest, it used to be a "showplace" for the sheriff. In the 1930s, this was where the local power brokers gathered to hunt, drink moonshine, and decide how to rule their kingdom.

"I could have it ready in a month," Charlie said. Charlie liked a challenge.

"I know an old boy," Forrest replied.

The "old boy" came out and we walked the mule path that led away from the house back into the forest. It was a single track, never wide enough for a car, following a foot-wide tributary of the Sandy Mush to a mountain spring. Beside the spring was a rock outcropping, and on top of the rock was a falling-down shack overgrown with bushes and volunteer trees.

"I grew up in that cabin," the man said. "Never had any electricity or nothing, but we had the spring."

"You're hired," I said.

In September, Forrest invited us to his apple-butter-making party. Mama Linda had started the tradition, and Forrest was keeping it up, with a few modifications. "I cheat," he admitted when he mentioned the event. "I add applesauce." Boiling down local apples into a hundred gallons of sugary brown mush had taken two days in Mama Linda's time, and Lord knows we no longer have that kind of patience. Forrest was planning to finish in five hours.

So we drove over to Forrest's one Saturday morning. He had a rambling single-story brick ranch house on Jarrett Farm Road, one ridge over from Angelwood. The front yard was a grass meadow, cut twice a year to make hay, and the backyard was forested. Behind the house sat the two-room cabin where Forrest had been born in 1930, one year after my own father. A friend had helped him move it after Mama Linda died. A dirt road—another part of the old stagecoach line—led down the ridge to a hidden grassy holler and a pond, where two dozen pickup trucks and SUVs were already parked.

A huge black pot as high as a man's waist was sitting on cinder blocks over an open fire, while a young man stirred the bubbling apple mixture with a big wooden paddle. Nearby was a covered picnic area, where a bluegrass band was picking and an entire hog was being spit-roasted over a second fire.

"I got the only outhouse in Madison County with a front porch," Forrest said, pointing toward the edge of the trees, and indeed he did. "If my wife knew how much money I'd spend down here," he joked, "she'd hit me in the head with a brick."

Luke spent the afternoon fishing from the dock—Forrest kept the pond well stocked—and Charlie and I spent our time meeting sheriffs, attorneys, farmers, businessmen, good old boys, and state government representatives. Forrest really did know everybody, and everybody loved Forrest. Charlie was so buzzed on moonshine from a mason jar by the time the sun broke behind the hills that I had to drive the family back to Asheville with two more mason jars Forrest wouldn't let us leave without.

"Ah, that's just nothing," Forrest said when I asked him about the abundance of liquor the next time he came by Angelwood. We'd put a deck on the back of the tobacco barn over-looking the stream, using old tobacco-drying rods we'd found in the barn for rails. "That's just a way of life. E. Y. Ponder himself used to sell that stuff out of the false bottom of his egg cart when I was a boy."

"Who's E. Y. Ponder?" I asked, making Forrest's eyes almost pop out of his head. He tipped back his Stetson and stretched out his ostrich-skin boots.

"That's my daddy's cousin," he said as he watched Luke playing in the water six feet below the deck. "Come around to the cabin behind my house and I'll show you."

I came around, of course, and Forrest's cabin did not disappoint. It was full of photos of Forrest's ancestors back to the Civil War and most of the things they'd ever owned, including the bed where Polly O'Dell was born and Mama Linda died. He had old soda cans, ancient tools, and a rough wooden box he handed me with special care.

"That's an authentic crooked ballot box used by Zeno Ponder," he said proudly.

Beginning in the 1930s, Zeno Ponder had risen from a local farming family to the head of the Democratic Party in Madison County. His brother Elmyas Yates (E. Y.) Ponder was the county sheriff. Another brother was the mayor of Marshall, the county seat. There were no large businesses in the area and no organizations besides the party. Nothing happened in Madison County—from hiring a schoolteacher to building a whiskey still—without a Ponder's approval.

We tend to think of moonshine as harmless. What's a little liquor among friends? For the first hundred years of Scotch-Irish craftsmanship, that's what it was: a quaint aspect of mountain culture, sold a jar at a time out of the false bottoms of egg carts.

When Prohibition was enacted in 1920, though, things changed. Overnight, the price of a gallon of moonshine quadrupled, and the criminal syndicates moved in. Moonshiners who had been bartering a few gallons a month now had standing orders for as much liquor as they could make, at mind-boggling prices.

The first thing to suffer was the traditional corn mash. It needed to ferment for a week before being distilled, and that was too slow for the hot market. So moonshiners started adding sugar to speed the process. The more sugar added, the quicker the fermentation. A week of waiting became two days. Before long, most moonshine was half sugar, at least. A story goes that a sugar executive wondered why they were selling more sugar in Buncombe County, North Carolina, than in New York City, so he caught the train to Asheville. He took one look at the tree-covered mountains, with their single-lane dirt roads and hidden hollers, and hopped right back on. He knew exactly where that sugar was going.

Sugar might not have made a tasty moonshine, but at least it wasn't poison. Soon moonshiners began to take other, less safe shortcuts. They used salvaged lead parts and old car radiators to build stills. They added lye, the scouring agent in soap, for extra "kick." One popular recipe was revealed to be mostly sugar, but also cornmeal, lye, tobacco, pokeberries, and soda. Unscrupulous producers burned a piece of wood, let it sit in harsh homemade hooch for a day, and claimed it was "aged bourbon," because the charred wood would turn the liquor brown. Aged bourbon sold for twice the price of unaged white whiskey.

The amount of liquor flowing out of the hills in those days was unfathomable. Millions of gallons of moonshine were making their way from Appalachia to cities throughout the

East and Midwest. The trade brought money to the mountains, but it also brought crime and a serious law enforcement presence. Before Prohibition, the United States government was busting two thousand illegal stills a year. By the end of Prohibition, they were busting more than that in every state in the South. And some of the operations were huge. Federal agents found eight thousand gallons of whiskey in Ingle Hollow, and the moonshiners had been tipped off and moved most of their stock before the raid. It was common to find an operation with a hundred stills or more. People hid these huge businesses in caverns, cellars, or secret rooms. One famous female moonshiner dressed as a man so she could slip into a secret distilling operation buried beneath her cabin every night.

It was those stories that made moonshiners into national legends: colorful characters who were part outlaw, part avenger against government overreach. Even in the mountains, the two conflicting views overlapped, creating a complicated legacy with the Ponders standing astride it, dominating both sides of the law. When Forrest Jarrett showed me his cabin, he pointed to an old black-and-white photo of a preposterously bearded man that was hanging on the wall.

"That's Popcorn Sutton," he said. Marvin "Popcorn" Sutton is the most famous moonshiner of all time.

He shifted his finger a few inches to the left, to a black-and-white photo of a man with an axe standing on top of what must have been forty staved-in moonshine stills. "That's Jesse James Bailey," Forrest said. Jesse James Bailey, E. Y. Ponder's predecessor as the sheriff of Madison and Buncombe Counties in the 1920s, was Prohibition's most notorious liquor buster, and one of the most famous and feared men of his era.

I didn't know any of this at the time. I didn't know Popcorn Sutton from Orville Redenbacher, or Jesse James Bailey from . . . the outlaw Jesse James. I didn't know the mountains, or liquor, or the long spiderlegs of history in these parts, or how those Prohibition moonshine traditions had come down to the current day, twisted and mangled and lovely in their way.

But with a guide like Forrest Jarrett, how could I resist learning more?

CHAPTER II

WHISPER MOUNTAIN

Charlie and I were developers at heart, and we bought a few other pieces of land around the same time we bought Angelwood. These were business opportunities, pure and simple. We planned to divide and sell the properties right away, as Dad had advised us so long ago.

Then Charlie found the real prize, seventeen miles from downtown Asheville: a four-thousand-foot mountain above an undeveloped holler accessible from a winding two-lane road. We took a little dirt path to the top, and I could see ten ridges without a single human development to mar the view. This was the summer of 2005, and most of the good land had been bought by wealthy people building second homes. This mountain was a rare unspoiled opportunity.

More importantly, it was Charlie's dream project: the chance to develop a one-of-a-kind green community of hiking trails, preserved woodlands, and high-end site-specific houses.

Angelwood was a fine little property. But Whisper Mountain, as I named it, would be the culmination of his life's work.

How could I refuse?

Especially when it was my dream project, too. After twenty-five years of staying home with the boys, Whisper Mountain was my chance to work side by side with my husband again, something I had missed so much. It was the project that would see us through our golden years: a community we could plan, build, sell, and nurture together for a decade or more, then retire to with the boys when the time was right.

It took a year to consolidate the property, which was broken up into fourteen different parcels, mainly in the hands of people whose families had held them for generations. It took another three months for Charlie and me to plan the community, laying out eighty parcels to sell undeveloped, with an option for us to design and build a home for the buyer. We wanted Whisper Mountain to be environmentally friendly, a place for reading, writing, painting, and relaxing, so we preserved heavily forested areas in conservation easements and laid out hiking trails. I don't think, in those first six months, we disagreed at all.

But once we started building, Charlie began to take control. "I know what I'm doing, Troy," he said with a sigh when I questioned his plans for the main road. "I've done this twenty times."

Or "Troy, I've been doing this for thirty years. Trust me."

Charlie didn't mean to insult me. When we started our development business in 1986, Charlie had treated me as an equal. Then I'd dropped out of the business to devote myself to the boys, a decision that allowed Charlie to keep working. He always loved me. He appreciated what I did. But now I could see what I'd sacrificed. Charlie no longer needed me as his business partner. I was his partner in the home, but at Whisper Mountain, he was the boss.

I don't blame Charlie. I know I'm not the only woman who has faced this issue. It's the way our society is structured. If you take two years away to care for your children, you're not serious about your career. If you take twenty years because those children have special needs, your career is dead. The men in power aren't interested in what you've learned or how you've grown. They smile and say you've done "the most important job in the world." Then they turn their backs on you because to them doing "the most important job in the world" means you're no longer qualified to do anything else.

I'm the expert. This is my thing. Let me handle this. I had heard these words from men all my professional life, but from Charlie—my husband, my love—it stung.

I took my disappointment and socked it away. I put my effort into Angelwood, where I could set the boys on the deck behind the tobacco barn or on the grassy slope beside the creek, where the shade from the trees kept them cool. Charlie and I put a paved road along the mule path to open up the back acreage. We platted building sites beyond the ridge, out of sight of the main house. But I didn't develop them. Angelwood had its own energy, a lazy flow like the meandering Sandy Mush, and I took my time. I had Forrest's contractor and his assistant take down the dilapidated gristmill by hand to preserve the stones. I started rehabbing the house. It was so old the walls were insulated with newspapers from the 1910s. The attic was filled with the Madison County tax ledgers for the first few years of the 1930s. There was a history here. I could feel it down to my toes, even if I wasn't quite sure what it was.

"My man quit," the contractor said one day when I pulled up in my ten-year-old Mercedes, the boys back in Asheville with Mom. It was a scorching-hot summer day, but along the Sandy Mush, the air was cool.

"What happened?"

"We saw an old man out behind the tobacco barn," the contractor said, "but when we went to talk to him, he was gone. Saw him again the next day, same thing. The third time we saw him, my man said that was enough. He wasn't working here no more. The place was haunted."

Forrest laughed when I told him the story. His uncle had been killed in the 1930s, he said, in a dispute over his brother's dogs butchering a few of his sheep. "He was a bad drunk," Forrest assured me when I was startled by the family infighting. "He had it coming."

"You think he's haunting the place?"

"Well, gosh no, Troy. What do you take me for?" He paused, adjusting his two-ton belt buckle. "Besides, he was killed on up around the corner anyway."

I spent two summers at Angelwood with the boys, as Charlie cleared a road up Whisper Mountain and used the harvested wood to build a gorgeous community center for the residents. He buried the power lines and utilities, engineered a beautiful stone gateway, and erected a spec home to serve as an office and advertisement. I urged him to stay on top of the brokers, since we had sold only fifteen lots out of eighty in two years, but Charlie wouldn't discuss it. He'd built Michael Dell's house. He'd developed award-winning projects in Austin. Whisper Mountain would sell, in the end, because it was the best-built and highest-quality development in Buncombe County.

I never stopped trying. I never stopped giving my opinion. But after a while, I felt like that mysterious ghost at Angelwood, an unwanted presence haunting a place that was no longer mine. My primary contribution to Whisper Mountain turned out to be landscaping: choosing shrubs and flowers, positioning stones. If Charlie had wanted to shunt me into stereotypical women's work, he couldn't have picked anything better. And he had no idea, at all, that he'd pushed me down.

Then we sold Angelwood, at the top of the market in 2008. That was my decision as much as Charlie's. We were offered double what we'd paid for the property. It was an offer we couldn't refuse, even if it broke my heart. Sitting on the deck with Marshall and Coulton on a quiet afternoon while Luke and his friends played in the water, feeling the history of the mountains as Forrest regaled me with stories, had felt like happiness. Now it was gone, and I had never spent a single night in the half-refurbished house.

I was lamenting the situation one afternoon with my friend Carol, who was visiting from Texas. Carol had largely given up the horses to become a flight attendant because she needed the health insurance. If anything, I should have been comforting her. But instead, she gave me the advice that changed my life: "If you want to be happy, Troy, you need a business of your own. You're never going to be happy as Charlie's assistant."

A business of my own. Not a hobby, not a property, but a moneymaking business.

It was as if thunder had struck. Of course that's what I needed. I had spent my entire life in the shadow of men: first Dad, now Charlie. I had accepted that role.

But I didn't want to be a man's sidekick. I wanted to be an entrepreneur. I'd wanted it since I was ten years old and Dad took me to my first sales seminars. I'd given Marshall and Coulton twenty-two years, and they would always be my first priority, but they were finally healthy enough, and supported enough, for me to focus on my own life. Why was I relying on Charlie?

I had $20,000 in a personal savings account, money I'd saved from selling the horses when I was leaving Texas. That was my "pin money." That was my opportunity to roll the dice and follow my dreams, for as long as the money held out. And I had a good idea what I wanted to do.

I wanted to make moonshine.

CHAPTER 12

FINDING FORREST

I can see how my decision might seem preposterous. After all, I was a forty-eight-year-old mother who had been raised in a strict religious household and had consumed maybe twenty glasses of alcohol in her entire life, mostly red wine. I was a Texas girl, born to the ranch. I was also a Vandy girl, the kind who wore pressed jeans and pearl earrings. What could I possibly know about distilling moonshine?

The short answer: Nothing. Nothing at all.

But I was confident, because I was an entrepreneur. I had founded a profitable horse show circuit when I was fourteen. I had cofounded a multimillion-dollar property development company. My special needs son was a bestselling author.

I wasn't naive. I knew how much hard work starting a successful business took. I crunched the numbers and knew my money wouldn't take me all the way to market, but I was confident it would take me far enough to create a brand. That's what I wanted to do: create a great line of whiskeys. If I had a good enough sample product, I could woo investors to help me scale up and bring it to market. And, ultimately, maybe, I could entice a large conglomerate to partner with me or to buy the brand and spread it all over the world.

I needed help. I needed *tons* of help. I wasn't afraid of that. I had always sought out help. It would take years of growth to be profitable, maybe a decade. I wasn't afraid of that either. I had the energy and desire; it had been building inside me. I had the business savvy. I could sell, darn it, and as Dad always told me, *If you can sell, Troy, you will never be hungry. You will always succeed.*

Most importantly, I had the right connection. When I was a little girl, I overheard Dad telling my brother, "The secret to success is using your resources—the people you know and their knowledge."

So I had the best resource of all: Forrest Jarrett.

The year before, Forrest and I had finally knocked heads over his moonshine. "Don't give me those white squeezings, Forrest," I told him one wintery day when he came by Angelwood with another pet 'n' poke in a quart jar. "I've got a pantry full already, and nobody will touch it. The stuff is awful."

"Well, sure it is," Forrest said. "That's nothing but the leavings."

Two days later, Forrest pulled up to the Big House, as he called my home in Asheville. I didn't realize he knew where I lived, but Forrest is resourceful. He knows everything. I looked at him skeptically when I saw the quart jar in his hand, but he said, "Trust me, Troy, it's the good stuff."

He winked and gave me another of his famous lines: "Found it in an old stump out on the Eleven Mile Road." Apparently, an old stump used to be the liquor store in northwest Buncombe County. You left your money, came back a few hours later, and found a jar.

I tried the "good stuff" out on my sister Trish. I mean, what are younger sisters for, right? She was pleasantly surprised, so I decided to serve it to the four women who were coming to my house that night for a meeting. I set out the jar of moonshine and some fruit juice I rummaged in my pantry, and to my surprise, those ladies drank the whole quart. By the end of the evening, we were all sipping straight moonshine from the jar. It was good: no burn, no foul taste, just smooth drinking. And the next morning, everybody felt wonderful. No hangovers, no regrets. And believe me when I say that like me, these ladies weren't the heavy-drinking types.

That reminded me of something I had heard Ross Perot, the Texas billionaire and maverick presidential candidate, say: "If you want to be successful, study an industry and find out what's missing."

I went straight to the local ABC (Alcoholic Beverage Control) store. In North Carolina, only ABC stores are allowed to sell hard liquor. I wanted to see how many brands of moonshine they carried. I found three, so I bought them. I sipped them. They were terrible. One tasted like nutmeg—on purpose!

Well, there it was: the hole in the market. White whiskey, a.k.a. moonshine, was an American tradition, born in the Appalachians. It had a two-hundred-year history, a romantic association with outlaws and home distillers, and a delicious flavor, perfect for sipping straight or mixing in cocktails. I didn't think of its cousins, scotch and bourbon, when I thought of the competition. I thought, *I can't believe people are drinking Russian vodka when we have a better American white spirit right here.*

I called Forrest Jarrett. I said, "Forrest, you've got to introduce me to your friends. I want to learn to make moonshine."

Forrest was quiet, maybe for the first time in his life. Then he laughed. "Troy," he said, "there is no way in hell those boys are ever going to talk to you."

I thought of my dad's wisdom: *You never get anything by giving up. No just means you haven't given them the information they need to say yes.*

I am nothing if not persistent. That was the secret of working with experts. You had to find them, but you also had to keep asking, because they always started out saying no.

So I set about stalking my friend Forrest. I called him every day. I brought my four boys (that includes Charlie) and a bowl of baked beans to the picnics and pig roasts down by his pond. Forrest had a breakfast group that met every Saturday. Sometimes it met at Turkey Creek Café, a small cinder-block building in "downtown Leicester," as Forrest insisted on calling the intersection of Highway 63 and Old Newfound Road, even though the only other businesses near the intersection were a tire store and a Spanish-language church. Mostly, it met at the Moose Café—"the Moose," as Forrest always barked—a diner next to the Western North Carolina Farmers Market.

The Moose served standard Southern fare, like biscuits, bacon, and a vegetable plate that included three fried items and no vegetables. (I have been to Southern diners that feature gravy in the "vegetable" options.) It was clean and friendly, and Forrest's table was right in the shadow of the five-foot stuffed-animal moose that graced the door. The regulars included Jerry Rogers, Forrest's best friend, who was, as Forrest tells it, "shirtless at his own high school graduation"; the district attorney of Buncombe County; a few young lawyers; an orthopedic surgeon; a used-car-lot owner; and Mr. Michell Hicks, the principal chief of the Eastern Band of the Cherokee Indians, whose reservation bordered Madison County. I heard tell of "the governor's lady" (a high-ranking aide, from what I could gather) attending a few times, but I never saw her. Mostly, it was the old boys' network, the one that had come out of the mountains. And me, of course, in my Ann Taylor shirts and pearls.

I should acknowledge that, as far as I know, Forrest Jarrett was never a moonshiner, nor had he ever dabbled in anything specifically illegal. In fact, he was by profession a lawman, an occupation he fell into almost by accident.

"When I come home from the service in Korea," he explained to me once, "Zeno Ponder sent word through my first cousin Marvin Ball that he'd meet me in hell before I'd get a job in Madison County."

Zeno's father and Forrest's grandfather were brothers, and they'd both been born on the land where Forrest lived now. After their father died, Forrest's grandfather had traded with Zeno's father for his half of the farm, and the Ponders were convinced the Jarretts had cheated them.

"Maybe we did, a little bit," Forrest admitted. "Fortunately my father was close friends with Jesse James Bailey, the famous still buster, who was by then head of detectives for the railroad and interested in hiring some good ol' mountain boys for his crew. And that's how I became a pistol-toter for the Norfolk and Southern." Forrest always described himself that way, as just an old pistol-toter for the railroad. "I was gone thirty-seven years and two weeks for the Norfolk and Southern, and I'm just happy to be home."

He turned and looked at me, with his bulging eyes and ever-present smile. "The only reason they hired me was 'cause I was so ugly. I mean, I was *pitiful*."

It was another favorite line, almost always followed by: "If I'd ever learned to read and write, I'da made something of myself."

This was clearly untrue. Forrest was, I will admit, not Hollywood beautiful, but he was one of the sharpest men I've ever met. He spent his first few years with the railroad as a union buster and got his big break when the CEO became convinced someone from the union was trying to assassinate him. He brought Forrest and a friend to Roanoke to be his personal bodyguards. Those were rough times in the mountains. The railroad had offered the best jobs around, but it was determined to break the unions, and I know for a fact Forrest drew his guns on an angry mob more than once. He worked just about every state in the Deep South, and every angle, no doubt, and by the time the unions made their peace, out of weariness, not victory, Forrest had worked his way up to head of the Norfolk Southern police force.

It was a political position more than law enforcement, and Forrest took to it like a duck to muck. He had a flatbed railcar turned into a twenty-four-foot barbecue smoker, and he hauled that smoker to the political picnics of every legislator from Mississippi to Ohio. He spent his last working years in Washington, DC, lobbying on behalf of the railroad industry. His crowning achievement was the 1990 passage of a law allowing railroad detectives to pursue criminal investigations across state lines. Strom Thurmond sponsored it, and Forrest pushed it through by getting "all [his] boys" to pester every senator with more than one hundred phone calls a day. Bush the elder signed the act into law with Forrest at his side, and the picture of them together now hangs in a place of honor on his wall of mementos in the house on Jarrett Farm Road.

Forrest retired soon after to the life of a gentleman influence peddler and pet 'n' poke aficionado, secure in his lasting contribution to train safety. There will never again be a power broker like Zeno Ponder in the mountains, but Forrest is about as close as the modern world will allow. He knows the governor, not just "his girl." In fact, he's known every North Carolina governor for thirty years. He has sat in the personal box of Heath Shuler at University of Tennessee football games (Shuler was a North Carolina congressman but quarterbacked at Tennessee) and hunted with a dozen high-ranking national political figures. The eleven-thousand-acre natural preserve that borders his property is the result of Forrest's considerable political connections. So was the preservation of the train depot in Marshall, North Carolina, that Charlie and I had admired on our first trip into the mountains.

"They're gonna tear down the Marshall station, Forrest," Mama Linda had told him in a panic near the end of her life. "They can't tear down that station. That's where Papa Olin caught the train to come court me down at Hot Springs."

So Forrest called the CEO of the Norfolk Southern, who got the railroad to sell the station to the town for a dollar. Then Forrest secured a government grant to rehab it into a live music venue. He turned eighty-eight last year, and he still goes every Friday night to oversee the fifty-fifty raffle (where half the money collected is won by the winning ticket) that pays for the free entertainment. The venue, just so you don't think the money was wasted, is legendary in the bluegrass community.

"When Jeb Bush is president," he told me once in his usual confident shout, "we're going to get Bobby Medford pardoned, because I know an old boy who is good friends with the man who drives Jeb's car."

Bobby Medford was the former sheriff of Buncombe County and an FOF: Friend of Forrest. He had been sentenced to fifteen years in federal prison for taking kickbacks to allow video poker machines in the back rooms of gas stations, pizza joints, and other rural shops in danger of going out of business without the additional income.

Was he guilty?

"Sure he was guilty," Forrest barked, "but so were other sheriffs in western Care-lina who had taken protection money from the video poker machine companies. Medford was the only one sent to prison. They made an example of him, because he was the only Republican."

Clearly the pardon scheme was going nowhere, but Forrest wasn't short of successes. "Twenty congressmen," he proclaimed, making the feather in his Stetson wobble, "have a jar of my moonshine sitting in their offices. I deliver it myself, and I can tell you, they are tickled pink to get it."

"Just give me a name, Forrest," I'd say whenever I could get a word in. "I won't tell anybody who's making your moonshine. I just want to see how it's done."

"No, Troy. I can't do it. It's not my place."

All this secrecy may seem foolish. After all, Forrest was driving around the county giving the stuff away. He was giving it to congressmen! Who could possibly care, especially now, long after the heyday of moonshine?

That fear is partially a holdover from darker days. Many of today's moonshiners learned their trade in the 1970s, when the Feds were trying to snuff out the last of the crime syndicate trade. By then, moonshine was out of favor, and most of the liquor went to "hooch joints" and "shot houses" in impoverished inner-city neighborhoods, where it was sold by the glass. Operations moved to large urban centers like Atlanta, where an illegal still blew up a house down the road from the tony Dunwoody Country Club in 1971. When the Feds investigated, they found Mafia ties and a pipeline straight to the African-American section of town. By then, both sides—the shiners and law enforcement—had mostly moved on to the more lucrative business of marijuana. Zeno Ponder's people used to dry it openly in the old tobacco barns, according to Forrest, and E. Y. Ponder used to run shipments in county cars. By the 1990s, though, the explosive growth of methamphetamine production in the mountains had made the old Ponder marijuana racket look quaint.

Still, there was danger in running liquor. Popcorn Sutton, the folk hero whose picture Forrest had on his cabin wall, had been running hooch since the 1970s. He became a legend after a documentary about his life, *This Is the Last Dam Run of Likker I'll Ever Make,* was released in 2002. He was arrested in 2008, around the time I was pestering Forrest for information. Despite being in his sixties and in poor health, Popcorn was sentenced to a year and a half in prison. He took his own life in March 2009, rather than serve his time.

Yes, Popcorn was caught with seven hundred gallons of moonshine, and I suppose the government was trying to make a statement. But the guy was sixty-two (and looked ninety-two); he was an Appalachian institution; he had cancer. It was the late 2000s, long after most of the world thought of moonshining as nothing more than a fascinating historical footnote, and the government was still willing to *kill* a moonshiner, if that's what it took. No wonder Forrest's connection didn't want to talk to me. For all I knew, the man was running a massive operation in a mountain holler that made Popcorn's last dam run of likker look like a trickle.

But if you know me, you know I kept at it. Forrest kept coming around, because we were good friends, and I kept saying, "I don't need a name, Forrest. You can blindfold me for the trip. You can muzzle me. I don't care. I just want to see it done."

"Troy," Forrest laughed, "I think you need a new hobby."

Eventually, though, Forrest wore down. "I got a name for

you, Troy," he said one day, and I knew he'd made a special trip
to see me because he didn't have a pet 'n' poke in the back of
his truck. "It's Jerry Rogers."

Jerry Rogers! The guy who graduated shirtless from high
school? The guy I'd been eating breakfast with every Saturday
for the past forty weeks?

"That's him," Forrest said, enjoying my shock. What are
friends for, if not pulling your chain? "Jerry's distilling tomorrow, and I convinced him to let you watch. But you better get
on over there, because he's liable to change his mind."

A while later, I asked Forrest why he was helping Charlie
and me so much. We were interlopers, out-of-staters, and so
different from his other friends. He didn't have to take us in,
but he did. Why, I wanted to know, was he willing to put his
reputation on the line?

He leaned back, puffed out his cheeks, and said, "When
we came down from our cabin, back when I was a boy, Papa
Olin and I would pass the empty cabins of the people who had
left. Those were hard times, the Depression, and poverty had
run every family out, all the way down the mountain to the
last cabin at Rector's Corner. My daddy said, 'You watch, Forrest. One day, good people will come back to the mountains.
It won't happen in my lifetime, but it will happen in yours.'"

Forrest looked out from beneath his Stetson, the yellow
one with the rattlesnake band, his eyes on the middle distance,
like he was looking at those empty cabins even now. "Lot of
rich people want to come out here and build a fence," he said.
"They don't want anything to do with us. But when I saw the
way you and Charlie treat those boys of yours, and how much
you love 'em, I knew you were good people. And that's when I
knew my daddy was right: good people will come back to the
mountains. They always do."

CHAPTER 13

THE COOKOUT

The end of Prohibition didn't mean the end of illegal Appalachian liquor. Outlaws had spent years creating a multimillion-dollar production and distribution network, and they weren't going to dismantle it simply because the government amended the Constitution (again) in 1933.

Fortunately for the moonshiners, lawmakers placed a heavy tax on the production of legal alcohol, providing plenty of room for illegal hooch to undercut the market. The heyday of moonshining was actually the 1950s and 1960s, when millions of gallons of hard spirits, mostly white whiskeys and fruit brandies, flowed out of the mountains. The government estimated that in the late 1960s more than one-third of the hard alcohol consumed in the United States was illegally produced. One-third! Not all of these spirits came from the Appalachians, of course, but the region where Virginia, North Carolina, Tennessee, Kentucky, and Georgia come together was the heart of the industry.

An essential part of this network was the "trippers," the drivers who ferried the moonshine from the isolated mountain regions to the professional middlemen in big cities. Willie Carter Sharpe was a tripper who led a caravan of ten cars out of the Virginia mountains three times a day in the 1930s. Willie used the main roads, relying on firepower more than guile, but by the 1950s the trippers of Western North Carolina were making use of the old logging routes abandoned when the local timber industry collapsed after World War II. The drivers jacked up their wheelbase and added suspension to clear stumps and navigate potholes in the dirt roads, and they modified their motors to give them more speed on the highways. Since they used the same mechanics as the federal officers—the local forces were run by men like the Ponders, if you know what I mean—the moonshine trippers could always make sure they stayed at least one modification ahead of the lawmen.

It was out of this tradition of souped-up cars and fast driving that NASCAR was born, and one of the most famous trippers of the era became one of the most famous early stock car drivers, Junior Johnson of Wilkesboro, North Carolina. The son of a moonshiner, Johnson quit running 'shine in 1955 to join the racing circuit and won fifty times in his career, earning the nickname "the Last American Hero." He parlayed that fame into a line of pork rinds and, in 2007, one of the first brands of legal, sugary moonshine.

Jerry Rogers's experience was more typical of a tripper from that era. Jerry was a half-breed, as Forrest lovingly (and cringeworthily) referred to him, part Cherokee, part white, and never fully accepted in either world. He'd grown up poor on Cherokee land and started running moonshine down to Georgia and over to Tennessee when he was fifteen. Eventually, the law caught up to him, and he was given a choice—go to jail or go to Vietnam. Jerry made the wrong choice. He chose Vietnam.

He came back torn up by Agent Orange. He didn't talk about the war, and as Forrest put it, he had spells. His skin would peel off in angry red slabs, and his joints burned. Even if he'd been capable of high-speed driving, this was the 1970s, and the moonshine business was dying. Part of the reason was the advances in law enforcement technique, such as the use of airplanes with infrared heat sensors to detect stills. Part was a switch to marijuana. The primary problem was the tax on man-ufacturers of liquor. It hadn't been raised since the 1950s, and after twenty years of inflation, its value was so low that there wasn't much room left to undercut the market. (The tax still hasn't been raised since the 1950s, not that I'm complaining.) Illegal liquor had become unnecessary outside of the poorest rural and inner-city neighborhoods, and because of the low profits and desperate clientele, the quality of the moonshine hit rock bottom.

Forrest helped Jerry out, securing him a job as a train-driving engineer on the railroad, but Jerry never regained what the jungle had taken from him. By the time I met him thirty years later, he was a storybook character, prone to mumbled mountain expressions that, for the life of me, I couldn't under-stand. I didn't know what to expect of his operation. Now that I was invited to see it, I realized it was probably going to be dirty, remote, rusty, and dangerous. So I convinced my sister Trish to come with me on the theory of safety in numbers. Trish and I were close, and we had a lot in common. She was always up for an adventure.

Turns out, Jerry lived in a tidy little house just outside Ashe-ville. I'm sure it had once been in the country, but now it was less than a quarter mile from a middle-class suburban neighborhood, near the end of a dead-end road. He had a vintage American muscle car in the driveway, no doubt similar to the one he'd used to run moonshine, and a yard full of gorgeous flowers. The car was Jerry's hobby. The flowers had been his wife's. She had died a couple years before, and Jerry was going to tend those flowers in her honor until the day he died.

So much for my mountain stereotypes.

The property was a little farm, similar to Forrest's in that it was wooded and sloped down in the back toward a pond. (Everything slopes around Asheville.) Jerry's distilling shed was across a grassy field, on the edge of the forest. It had a garage door he kept open to vent the liquor fumes, and I could see his rig from a hundred feet away, although it wasn't visible from the road.

"Any problems with unwanted attention?" I asked, thinking of the nearby neighborhood.

"Just the bar," he said.

Jerry got a call about a disturbance from a neighbor one afternoon, and he came running down to check out the problem. He had expected robbers or troublemaking teens; instead, there was a "bar" lying in his grassy field. The bear had eaten half a barrel of fermented mash, lurched away from the shed, and passed out drunk.

"She was right there," Jerry said, pointing to the grassy field as he unlocked the garage door.

Inside, Jerry's setup was straight out of the 1950s. He had an old propane burner and a fifteen-gallon cook pot for heating mash. Mash, the basis of whiskey, is a mixture of corn, water, yeast, and whatever other grains you want to add for flavor. Jerry used a bag of feed corn from the local farm supply store. The kernels were broken to dust and intended for chickens. The bag was stamped "Feed for animals." I could see leaves and grass coming out with the corn as he poured it into the cook pot, but Jerry didn't bother to clear them.

"It'll cook off," he said.

He added water to cover the corn, then turned the propane burner pretty high. I could see blue flames licking the bottom of the pot.

"Start stirring," he said, handing Trish a wooden paddle.

The mash looked like yellow oatmeal. The paddle would occasionally bring up a brown leaf, or something else that had fallen into the bag at the processing plant, but Jerry wasn't worried.

"Everything will cook out," he said again.

The only thing that mattered, according to Jerry, was that the mash didn't stick to the bottom of the pot and burn. So my sister and I took turns stirring slowly and deeply, switching off when we got tired. After an hour, Jerry turned off the burner and poured the mash into a plastic barrel to cool. It looked smoother and creamier than when we started, but otherwise, it seemed pretty much the same.

"Why an hour?" I asked.

Jerry shrugged. "Because that's what my daddy told me."

After an hour of cooling, Jerry added a fifty-pound bag of sugar and a block of store-bought yeast about the size of four sticks of butter. I was fascinated. My sister was appalled. She worked in food and beverage purchasing, first at Whole Foods in Texas, and for the last five years at the Biltmore Estate. This operation was clearly not up to health code, and it wasn't very precise, either. But it was honest-to-God moonshining.

"What do we do now?" I asked as Jerry put a lid on the barrel. I guess that was meant to keep away the "bars."

"We wait."

I looked at the equipment. There weren't any gauges or thermometers. It was just a plastic barrel. "How long?"

"Until it stops bubbling."

I stared at him, waiting for more. Jerry just looked at me.

"About five days," he said eventually. "Maybe a week."

Trish and I came back to the shed the next day to check on the mash. It was autumn, and the leaves were golden orange. With the little pond and the fall flowers, Jerry's property was the perfect place to waste a quiet day. I imagined Luke fishing there, then remembered he was a freshman in high school and he'd given up fishing in favor of girls. Jerry's operation was as quiet as the pond, with the activity nothing more than large bubbles rising lazily through the yellow oatmeal mash. The yeast had looked like a solid block of powder, but it was actually millions of tiny animals. They were eating the corn and cane sugars and emitting waste, a process commonly known as "passing gas." The by-product of all those gaseous emissions was alcohol. When the gas passing (technically fermenting) stopped, the mash was ready. I came back three times to check on the mash, and each time it was bubbling. By the fourth day, the bubbles were noticeably smaller. When the mash stopped bubbling, Jerry told me, it would be ready.

On the fifth day, Coulton had a respiratory infection, and I couldn't get away. The boys were much healthier than in Texas, but they were still fragile, and my son needed me.

A few days later, I drove back to Jerry's farm. The mash was gone. Jerry had distilled it into white squeezings while I'd been caring for Coulton.

I was disappointed. "Why didn't you wait for me?"

He shrugged. "When it's ready, it's time," he said, something that might have been mountain wisdom. He handed me a quart jar of clear liquid, just like the ones Forrest gave out in his pet 'n' pokes. I tasted the white whiskey. It was awful.

Six months, I thought as I drove the fifteen minutes back to my house. *I waited six months for this?*

I learned years later that Jerry wasn't Forrest's primary supplier. "I got an old boy has an operation like a hospital," he admitted, by which I assume he meant high-tech and sterile. I guess he'd been putting me off when he told me about Jerry, but Forrest had actually done me a favor that day. I hadn't learned much about moonshine. I hadn't even seen Jerry distill his mash. But I'd learned something more important: distilling wasn't hard. Anyone could make moonshine.

I just needed to figure out how to make it good.

CHAPTER 14

ALABAMA CLYDE

I suspected Forrest was holding out on me. Jerry Rogers might have been making his paint peeler, but someone else must have been making the good stuff. So I went after Forrest hard for another name. Aren't we friends, Forrest? Don't you trust me?

"I don't know, Troy," he said with his sly smile. "Are you the kind of friend who still comes round after they've got what they wanted?"

It was a friend of Rosie, my best friend from college, who gave me the tip I needed. He and a group of buddies went on an annual deer-hunting trip in Alabama. The hunting guide at the camp distilled his own liquor, and Rosie's friend thought it was pretty good.

I called, and of course the hunting guide hung up on me. I tried again. No, he didn't want to share his distilling method. In fact, he was not pleased someone was talking. I thought, after my first few calls, that I might get some hunting privileges revoked.

Turns out, the hunting guide—I'm going to give him the fake name Clyde, because I had a great-uncle named Clyde who rode in the rodeo, and they looked a lot alike—wasn't worried about law enforcement. He was making small batches to give away to friends and clients, like the backwoods version of suburban dads and their garage beer-brewing operations. Jerry's fifty-five-gallon barrel of mash produced five gallons of moonshine; Clyde was only producing a gallon at a time, to be shared around the campfire.

No, it wasn't the sheriff Clyde feared. It was his wife. She didn't know about his hobby.

Who am I, though, if not a salesman? I find something I want, and I don't stop until I get it. So I'm sorry, Clyde, you can't say no, because if you do, I'm going to keep calling—and selling you on myself—until you say yes.

Eventually, Clyde surrendered. He wouldn't distill for me, but he said I could come to the hunting camp and record him as he explained his distillation methods, as long as I agreed to film nothing above his boots.

I went down in early December 2008, about four months after watching Jerry Rogers's bubbling mash. I hated leaving the boys overnight, but I was confident they were in good hands with Mom and Charlie. At this point, my hesitation was more about giving myself permission to follow my dreams than Marshall's and Coulton's physical needs. Marshall's answer, when I asked him if he minded my starting a distillery, had helped ease that tension.

Marshall knows dear fine thought rooms sweetly with Mama.

Still, leaving Marshall and Coulton overnight was a big step. I couldn't help but feel a little selfish for putting myself before the boys, even though I knew it's important for women to be selfish sometimes. We're expected to give, give, give for our family and friends, but a balanced life means giving to yourself as well.

I thank God Charlie always understood that and never used guilt to keep me home.

The hunting camp, of course, was no vacation resort. In fact, it was quite primitive: a clapboard bunkhouse with electricity but no hot water, and the kind of thin old mattresses only men could enjoy. Moonshine is thought of as mountain dew, but this was the Piedmont region, full of low hills and canebrakes. Clyde and I sat on the front porch of the bunkhouse, rocking in old chairs, talking about our lives, and sipping his quite lovely homemade whiskey. Evening comes early in winter, and the sunlight shot through the pines at eerie angles. I could hear scuffling in the woods, even though the snakes were hibernating, while Clyde cooked collards, pork chops, and corn bread in an iron skillet. It wasn't the best place for a woman alone, I suppose, but Clyde was a hell of a cook.

And what did his wife think, I wondered, about her husband's being alone at the camp with a blonde? I didn't ask. I assumed she didn't know. I was just happy to get through a night on that decrepit cot.

The next morning, after another hearty meal, Clyde took me to the side room in the barn where he kept his distilling equipment. A propane burner was the heat source, just like in Jerry's operation. A five-gallon pressure cooker—perfect for beef stew, too!—was for cooking the mash. Use white corn, Clyde insisted. That was the key. Whole-kernel white corn.

"Why white corn?"

"Don't know." Like Jerry's insistence on cooking for exactly one hour, it was handed-down wisdom. It was simply what an old-timer had told him.

The fermentation barrel was similar to Jerry's. Like Jerry, Clyde added sugar, but he didn't add yeast. Clyde relied on the wild yeast in the air to start the fermentation process. It took about fourteen days.

Once it was fermented, Clyde put the mash back in the pressure cooker. "It seals airtight," he said.

He removed the pressure cooker's regulator, leaving a hole in the middle of the lid. (So much for the seal.) He walked to the corner and retrieved a piece of thin copper pipe. The pipe ran for nine inches, then bent ninety degrees and continued for another nine feet. The short end fit snugly into the hole in the pressure cooker lid. As I filmed his hands, Clyde clamped the pipe into position with nuts and bolts. The long end stuck out at a right angle, parallel to the ground. As the fermented mash heated, vapor would rise into the pipe.

There was no way to set a temperature. There were no gauges. How did he know when the heat was right?

He grabbed the exposed copper pipe, right above the pressure cooker. "You want it hot, but not too hot. It should be uncomfortable, but not too painful to hold."

If it was too hot or too cold, Clyde adjusted the flame. The right temperature was vital, he said, to getting the right taste.

"How did you come up with that method?"

He shrugged (while I filmed his boots). "Practice, I guess."

He walked to another corner and retrieved a long white PVC pipe. The pipe was eight feet long and capped on both ends. The caps had holes in the middle so Clyde could slide the PVC around the long section of copper piping. A hole on the top allowed him to add cold water with a hose. The water cooled the copper pipe, causing the vapor inside to condense into liquid. If the temperature of the water and mash were right, a thin trickle of clear liquid—white whiskey—would run out the far end of the copper pipe. Clyde caught it directly in a jar. Or his mouth. Or whatever vessel he wanted.

Everything mattered, he explained as he disassembled the pieces and hid them back in plain sight. The type of corn. The wild yeast. The length of the copper pipe. The way it was angled, about five degrees, so that the condensation would drip out slowly, not pour. If the trickle was too fast, he could adjust the burner. If it was too slow, he could open a spigot in the PVC pipe to pour out the old, warmed water and replace it with cold. He didn't have any gauges, but he had practical methods for testing his process, and he had a mixture of old wisdom and personal experimentation that left nothing to chance.

I could taste the care in the finished product Clyde gave me to take home. It was smooth, without the oily alcohol smell and chemical burn of Jerry's firewater. It really did taste good.

But it wasn't quite there. Clyde was going on feel, and with moonshine, you can taste something as small as half a degree of temperature. He was using store-bought corn and wild yeast, and his cooling method was approximate, not precise. Clyde could distill a sellable product, especially after the first few shots went down, but there was no way, with his setup, he could make a consistently great whiskey.

And, honestly, he wasn't even making whiskey. Whiskey is a technical term. By definition, it is alcohol created from the fermentation of grain. Jerry and Clyde were adding cane sugar to speed the fermentation process. I didn't realize it at the time, but this is the primary problem with the other moonshines on the market. The recipes have been passed down from fathers or even grandfathers, and they all use sugar, because sugar was the basis of the cheap moonshine that started being produced in the 1920s. You have to go back more than a hundred years, to the way moonshine was made before Prohibition, to capture the true essence of the Appalachian version of Scotch-Irish whiskey.

What Jerry, Clyde, Junior Johnson, Popcorn Sutton, and all the others were distilling was rum, not whiskey. Or more accurately, a cross between whiskey and rum.

But mostly rum.

It didn't matter. I wasn't interested in copying Clyde's recipe, or even his technique. I was trying to learn what was important to moonshiners, and why, so that I could make my own white whiskey.

"I'll send you a bottle, as soon as I'm satisfied," I told Clyde as I was packing to leave.

"Oh God, please don't," he said.

The hunting camp couldn't receive mail, so Clyde used a local store. His wife usually picked up his packages. He didn't want to have to explain to her why he was receiving whiskey from some woman in North Carolina.

I ended up driving back to Alabama three years later with a bottle from my first legal batch of Troy & Sons white whiskey. I gave it to Clyde at the hunting camp, along with a poster we'd made to promote the brand. It was a picture of me, in a white blouse, blue jeans, and knee-high boots, walking through a field of grain. My friend's husband still hunts at the camp, and he told me the poster is still hanging in the bunkhouse.

So I made it. Every girl's dream. I was a hunting camp pinup . . . at fifty-two.

CHAPTER 15

BLOCK AND TACKLE

Some mountain people call moonshine block and tackle, because if you walk a block after drinking it, you're likely to tackle someone. They also call it white mule, catdaddy, panther piss, tangleleg, and about a hundred other things, but I digress. My point is that when it came to my making moonshine, it seemed to be all blocking so far. It was Christmas 2008; it had been a year since I started throwing myself on Forrest Jarrett's mercy, not to mention the two decades I'd spent raising Marshall, Coulton, and Luke. I was finally ready to do some tackling. I walked in the door from Alabama, hugged all four of my boys (Charlie got one too, of course), and declared, "I need to build a moonshine still."

It was my Christmas gift to myself.

Charlie laughed. "That's illegal, Troy."

Um . . . what did he think I'd been doing for the past twelve months? Writing a magazine article?

"And besides," he said, "where are you going to put it?"

I hadn't thought about it, but there was one logical place. "In the basement," I said.

"Troy," Charlie said, suddenly serious, "you are going to blow the house up."

He might have been right. As I now know, cooking mash releases vapor, and the vapor builds up over time. If you don't have adequate ventilation, you really can blow up your house, garage, or business.

I was not so wise back in early 2009, though, and I was determined. I'd been talking about this for a year. I'd traveled to *south Alabama*. And Charlie still didn't realize I was serious? He should have known me better by then.

I went to the store and bought a five-gallon pressure cooker. I needed Charlie to take the gauge off the top and modify it for the condenser pipe, because he was an engineer, and I am not as handy with tools. He laughed me off, so I started carrying the pressure cooker around the house. If we were changing the boys' diapers, I'd put the pressure cooker beside the changing table. If Charlie and Luke were watching television, I'd put the pressure cooker on the couch beside them. I'd keep it on the bathroom counter when we were getting ready for bed and on my nightstand for when he woke up to take care of the boys. That pressure cooker *haunted* Charlie. He couldn't get away from it.

He only agreed to help me, though, when it became clear that I was ready to turn it into a moonshine still by myself.

Now, that terrified him.

So we went to Lowe's together to buy the gauges, copper pipe, and nuts and bolts needed to create a seal. I was testing out a ten-foot length of copper pipe, seeing how easy it was to bend into shape (not easy), when I noticed a sales assistant hovering nearby. He was stick thin with a long gray beard, overalls, and an impressive shuffle. He shook his head and muttered, "I don't want to know what y'all are doing," as he shuffled off.

Nah, I thought. *I'm being paranoid.*

We took everything home and tried to attach the pipe to the top of the pressure cooker, but it was hard to get a seal. We called Luke down, since he was pretty handy, but he wasn't sure how to do it, either. Eventually, Charlie called our neighbor, and with the right tools we got the fittings to work. I'm pretty sure he didn't figure out what we were trying to do. I might have mentioned something about Luke's science fair project . . .

Finally, by March, I had my still nestled in my corner in the basement. The next step was creating the right mash, and the right mash meant the right corn. I didn't know at the time how vital corn was to whiskey, but if Alabama Clyde felt so strongly about his whole-kernel white corn, I knew it must be important. But where was I going to find quality corn? I certainly wasn't going to use Jerry Rogers's animal feed.

Fortunately, that's when Charlie stepped up.

No, not my husband Charlie.

My loud-and-proud gal pal Charlie.

As I mentioned before, my mother lived with us in Asheville. She spent most of her time helping Trish and me with our children, but she had her own daily routine, too. This routine involved frequent visits to her favorite neighborhood restaurant, Tomato Jam. Tomato Jam was owned and operated by a lesbian couple. Rebecca, who ran the front of the house, was quiet and well mannered, like a Vanderbilt girl. Charlie, the cook, was not.

Charlie was big. I'm not talking about size, although she *was* tall, muscular, and barrel shaped. Charlie had short salt-

and-pepper hair, tattoos, a wardrobe that seemed to consist entirely of checked chef's pants and Chacos, and a big personality that stomped on fussy manners and dominated the room from her open kitchen. Every time she saw a new customer coming in the door, she'd call out in her booming voice, "Welcome to Tomato Jam. How y'all doing today?"

Charlie also made the best grits bowl in town, which is exactly what it sounds like: a bowl of grits topped with eggs, bacon, onions, Brussels sprouts, mushrooms, or whatever else you wanted. Grits, of course, are coarsely ground corn. I hope I didn't have to tell y'all that.

I'm not sure how moonshine came up, other than that Charlie and I both liked talking, and she loved Coulton and Marshall. I loved her for it, because nobody complained about the boys' being loud or dirty when Charlie was around. Nobody even gave us a dirty look, because they knew Charlie wouldn't allow it. Somehow, one day, we started talking about grits, and she told me the secret was the corn. She got hers from a local farmer named John McEntire who grew a rare heirloom white corn called Crooked Creek. He even hand-ground it right on his farm.

What could be more perfect for a traditional heirloom North Carolina whiskey, I thought, than traditional heirloom North Carolina corn?

I called John McEntire the next day. "Sure I got white corn," he said in a mild Southern accent. "How much you need?"

"About a hundred pounds."

"Well, I've got it whole kernel, or I can grind it for you, rough or smooth."

I knew Clyde liked whole kernels, but I wasn't ready to take that as a given, so I said, "Better make it a hundred pounds of each."

"Oh, law," he said. "Are you that woman wants to make whiskey?"

I laughed. Charlie must have gotten to him first, but I preferred to think western Carolina was so small word got around. "That's me," I said.

John McEntire chuckled back. "Well," he said, "I tell you what. Why don't we trade corn for whiskey?"

We set up a time to meet a week later, and I thought I'd finally tackled the last block keeping me from my dreams. But one thing I've learned about life: it will always surprise you, and often in the worst possible way.

CHAPTER 16

SHAKEN

Coulton wasn't well the next morning. His breathing was labored, and he was lethargic. When I put on his favorite song, 311's "Amber," a song that had elicited an enthusiastic response a thousand times in a row without fail, he wasn't smiling and rocking back and forth. As much as Coulton's energy can frustrate me, I know when he is banging drawers or vocalizing loudly, his physical condition is strong. That's a great comfort, since he's unable to communicate any other way.

The health care worker arrived as scheduled, but I couldn't leave. I was already fighting guilt for being away from the boys, even though I knew my starting a business was healthy for all of us. I spent the morning rubbing Coulton's back to loosen his chest, holding him in my lap, and monitoring his breathing. Charlie and I gave him oxygen, as we had many times over the years, but by the afternoon, he was noticeably worse.

We took him to the hospital. This was only the third time

in the six years we'd been in Asheville that Coulton had been hospitalized. That may sound like a lot, but in Austin he'd been hospitalized twice a year. I suspected pneumonia, and I knew that meant a week in the hospital at least. Coulton was seventy-eight pounds fully clothed, and his body wasn't strong. I figured he would struggle for a few days, then gradually get better. He always did.

But a few hours after arriving in the ER, the doctors sat Charlie and me down with grim news. Coulton had developed acute respiratory distress syndrome (ARDS). Fluid was building in his lungs. He had no way to clear the congestion, and it was getting harder for him to breathe.

I started crying. I knew ARDS. A neighbor in Texas had been diagnosed with it. He had been in his early forties, a marathon runner in great shape. He almost died.

If a healthy man in the prime of life barely beat it, what chance did Coulton have?

I watched my boy on his hospital bed, a breathing tube down his throat. I held his hand as he tried to inhale. He didn't look at me, but his body shook. He couldn't catch his breath, and he didn't understand why. He gasped, choking on the tube. He caught my gaze, and his eyes looked terrified. My poor son was terrified. A few minutes later, the doctors put him into an induced coma.

I couldn't leave him. I spent every minute with Coulton, sitting at his bedside. For two weeks, the hospital sent Charlie and me home every night at eleven, but every morning at six, we were back at Coulton's side.

My only break was lunch at Tomato Jam, a block from the hospital. Every day I would walk there for a sandwich, and every day Charlie would yell from her kitchen, "How's my boy?"

And every time, I would break down in tears. Charlie would

come out from behind the counter to engulf me, and I would sob in her arms. I couldn't speak, I was crying so hard.

There was nothing to say. Coulton was in a coma and getting weaker by the day. He couldn't get enough oxygen, so his body was dying. He couldn't expel enough carbon dioxide, so it was building up and suffocating his cells. Every few days, the fluid would cause one of his lungs to rupture, and the doctors would drive a spike into his side to release the pressure. This happened five times in five weeks, and each time the doctors told us the solution was temporary, that Coulton was getting worse and they couldn't keep driving sharp metal into his sides.

After six weeks, I went home for a day to rest, while Charlie and his parents took over at the hospital. Charlie's parents had driven from Texas, fourteen hours straight through the night, as soon as they heard about Coulton. They were like that. Even though they didn't live close, they were always ready and willing when we needed them most.

When I got home, Luke didn't know what to say. He was fifteen. It was hard enough to navigate teenage life without a dying brother. I didn't know what to say to him, either. Life is unfair sometimes, I guess, but he already knew that.

"Marshall loves Coulton," Marshall wrote on his alphabet board. "Are we thinking the end?"

Marshall doesn't often make facial expressions or control his body language. He can't look me in the eyes to let me know he is with me. He looked as calm at that moment as he did every minute of every day. What was he thinking? How did he feel?

"Don't worry," he wrote. "Love heals the good man."

I went back to the hospital. Coulton's carbon dioxide was reaching fatal levels. His lungs were wearing out. They couldn't take another puncture without collapsing completely. He hadn't moved or opened his eyes in weeks. His eyelids didn't even flutter when I played the song "Amber," his favorite thing in the world. The doctors were talking about other options. I could hear them saying it was wait for major organ failure or pull the plug, and I couldn't face either. I went for a grits bowl.

"How's my boy?" The words still echo in my heart, exactly the way Charlie yelled them when I walked in the door.

"How's my boy!"

He's not good, Charlie. He's not good. And you'd think I had cried all my tears, but they kept coming, especially when Charlie wrapped me in her arms and wouldn't let go.

After five weeks, Coulton's throat was destroyed. He needed a tracheotomy to insert the breathing tube directly into his neck. I doubted he would survive the surgery, because he was so weak. The doctors doubted, too. But a successful trach, they said, would give him more time.

"If he wakes up now," I asked, "will he be the same?"

"There's nothing to indicate permanent damage."

Charlie and I talked it over. We were in agreement. We had to try everything. It was Friday. We scheduled the surgery for first thing Monday morning.

Charlie put me in the car that night in a daze. I didn't want to go, but I needed to tell Luke and Marshall what was happening. I needed to hug my other two sons. I needed to pray. We were almost home when the thought struck me.

"I have to call Dr. Dejournett!"

Dr. Leon Dejournett had treated Coulton and Marshall in the past. He was a skilled pediatric surgeon but probably the most unorthodox doctor I have ever met. He didn't explain himself well, and his bedside manner sometimes felt dismissive. Charlie and Dr. Dejournett had butted heads on a previous hospital stay, in fact, because the doctor didn't seem interested in Charlie's opinion. I understood. Charlie was proud, and he always fought with a passion for Coulton and Marshall.

But I believed in Dr. Dejournett. He was fearless; if anyone could think of another option for Coulton, it would be him. And I had overheard a nurse saying he was going to be on call that night.

Charlie was sympathetic but unconvinced. "There's nothing he can do, Troy," he said gently. "Don't torture yourself."

But I had a feeling. I can't describe it any better than that. I always counted on the best experts. I always listened to them. I needed to talk to Dr. Dejournett. So as soon as we got home, I called the nursing station.

"Coulton is still in the hospital?" Dr. Dejournett said in surprise when I finally reached him. Dr. Dejournett had seen Coulton at the beginning of his stay, before going on vacation and then rotating to another building on his return. "Meet me in his room."

It was almost midnight, but Charlie and I got in the car and drove back to the hospital.

Dr. Dejournett was already there. He had been told about the scheduled surgery. He knew as well as I did Coulton probably wouldn't survive.

"We have one other option," he said, "if you're willing to trust me."

I could feel Charlie pull back, but I believed. "Do what you think is best," I said.

Charlie nodded grimly. "Do it," he said softly.

Dr. Dejournett pulled the curtain to hide Coulton, but Charlie and I maneuvered to where we had a view through a narrow opening. I watched as Dr. Dejournett got a flat wooden board about two feet wide and slid it under Coulton's back. Then he climbed on the bed, got down on his knees, and straddled Coulton, whose weight had dropped to sixty pounds. As

I watched, Dr. Dejournett lifted Coulton slowly, as if he was going to hug him, and then pounded him violently against the board. He lifted and pounded him again and again, until I thought Coulton must be shattered inside. Then he stopped, looked at the monitor, and stepped off the bed. He pulled back the curtain.

"What was that?" I demanded.

"I gave him the Dejournett Shake," he said. "He's on a regular ventilator now. We're taking him out of the coma. Coulton's going to be fine." Then he strutted down the hall, without looking back.

We canceled the surgery. We stayed until the wee hours, holding Coulton's hand.

The next morning, when I put on 311's "Amber," Coulton's eyes popped open, and he started jerking his head and blinking in excitement, as he always had. By slamming him repeatedly against the board, Dr. Dejournett had forcibly expelled the carbon dioxide trapped in his chest and loosened the blockage in his lungs.

Five days later, we took Coulton home. Marshall was waiting, as serene as always. Luke, my teenager, might have cried. And there was my Coulton, as healthy as he'd ever been, rocking out to his favorite song. I watched him closely for two more weeks, until I was sure Marshall had been right: Coulton wasn't leaving us. Love heals the good man.

I called John McEntire. I had forgotten to tell him I wasn't coming. "I'm sorry, John," I said. "Is there any way I can still get that corn?"

"I understand, Troy," he said kindly. "Come on down whenever you feel comfortable. I have two hundred pounds of white corn waiting for you."

PART III

Peaceful Valley Farm

CAN WE SEE MEARLY SOMBER COLORS?

GREATLY EACH SEASON COMES

CLEARLY HAVING GREAT BEACHES

IRREVERENTLY, MARVELOUSLY

NEARING THE BROUGH OF GOOD GOD.

BE A REALIZER OF GREAT SEASONS,

FOR YOU WILL REALIZE MY HARMONY

NEEDS SEASONS,

AND GOOD GOOD GOD

GIVES SEASONS TO FREE.

CHAPTER 17

CROOKED CREEK

John McEntire's farm is forty minutes east of Asheville, the opposite direction from Whisper Mountain, Madison County, and "the Earl of Leicester" Forrest Jarrett. Although the farm is just south of Mount Mitchell, the highest peak in the eastern United States, this isn't mountain country. The highway out of Asheville curves downward through the Pisgah National Forest, offering stunning views on damp days of clouds in the valley below, but for the entire drive you know you're headed down. The mountains get smaller and rounder until finally it occurs to you that for the last ten minutes they haven't been mountains at all. They are foothills, green and forested, unassuming like ocean waves far out from shore.

The exit off Interstate 40 is rural, with only a single gas station. The main road goes to the small town of Old Fort, North Carolina, population 908, but the road to John McEntire's farm cuts right, unmarked except for a handwritten sign pointing the way to the Baptist church. That's how it's always been in the valley forged by Crooked Creek. It isn't remote, but it's out of the way. You would never come upon it just passing through. The only reason you'd go there is if that's where you meant to go.

The McEntires have been in the valley for seven generations. As early as the 1850s, they were listed as one of twelve families living there, farming the bottomlands near the creek and milling the trees on the hills. The residents of the valley kept to themselves, not out of ethnic or religious clannishness, but because there was no place nearby worth visiting, and everything they needed could be traded for in Old Fort. They had claimed the best arable land in a sparsely populated region, and they were bound to each other by their location, their Baptist church, and the one crop they all farmed, Crooked Creek corn.

Nobody knows where the corn came from. John McEntire heard it came from Tennessee, making a reverse migration east over the mountains. By the 1880s, everyone in the valley was growing it. The plant was tall—twelve feet, when most cornstalks were about seven—and grew only one ear per plant, as opposed to the usual four or five. That one ear was much bigger than standard corn, with large white kernels. It's unclear whether the farmers found this corn superior or whether it was simply what they had. About half the corn was traded, and most of the rest was eaten by the families and their livestock. John McEntire ate Crooked Creek corn bread dipped in that morning's fresh milk almost every day before catching the bus to school. He often ate that corn bread for dinner, too.

While the families farmed separately, one family was tasked with storing the seed corn from each harvest, so that everyone in the valley would have enough to plant the next season. Four generations ago, that task fell to the McEntires, and they have diligently protected Crooked Creek corn ever since, even as the variety fell out of favor. The stalks were too tall, wasting all that growing energy. The single ear per plant meant yields per acre were small. The trend in farming was for shorter stalks that produced more ears. As modified and commodified farming took over the industry, the Crooked Creek farmers and their heirloom plants couldn't compete. Many valley residents switched to Monsanto-style engineered corn, and then most quit growing corn altogether. Small-scale farming wasn't viable anymore.

By the year 2000, John McEntire was the last person on earth growing Crooked Creek corn. He wasn't growing it commercially, though. Although he had lived his whole life on his family farm, John wasn't a professional farmer. For most of his career, he'd been a schoolteacher, like his wife. In his spare time, he carried on the family traditions. He milled wood with a fifty-year-old hand-fed band saw, raised chickens and goats, and grew ten acres of his family's heritage corn in the bottomlands alongside Crooked Creek, where seven generations had grown it before him. Every year he saved enough seed corn for another ten acres. He milled most of the rest, with either his grandfather's hand-cranked grinder or, if an order was large enough, the electric gristmill he kept in a screened room attached to a storage shed.

No one was more surprised than John McEntire when the foodies in Asheville discovered his corn. I have no doubt they were sold first by the story, although John is still unsure how they heard of him. They kept coming because the corn was delicious. Once I started making moonshine with it, I had some tested at the agricultural laboratory at the University of Tennessee. The researcher was astonished. He had never heard of Crooked Creek corn, and he had never seen anything like it.

The corn had by far the highest fat content of the more than one hundred corn varieties the laboratory had tested. I'm not a food scientist; I don't know how that affects cooking, tasting, and milling. All I know is that it makes a fantastic whiskey.

That realization was a year in the future, though. When I went out to John's farm for the first time in April 2009, all I had was my friend's recommendation and the memory of a delicious bowl of grits. The first thing I noticed, apart from how quiet and empty the last few miles had been, was a rickety pile of half-sawed trees and knotty timber in the muddy low ground near the creek to the left of the road. Turned out the pile of scraps was John McEntire's tilted old sawmill, with the debris of a hundred years of milling strewn haphazardly about.

On the other side of the road, a gentle hill sloped upward toward the tree line. A red barn with peeling paint and spaces between the slats hugged the road, looking like it might tilt too far at any moment and collapse into my lane. Beside the barn was a redbrick silo, the mortar cracked. Behind the barn, a gravel road meandered most of the way up the hill. The hillside was clear-cut but crowded with eight or nine little sheds and outbuildings, seemingly built at random over the last half century. The whole farm seemed knocked together. There wasn't a straight line or piece of level ground anywhere in sight.

PEACEFUL VALLEY FARM, proclaimed a handmade sign by the side of the road.

I pulled into the circular drive just past the barn. John came out of his house, and a large black dog jumped up from the shade to follow him. John was, in many ways, the exact opposite of the old pistol-toter Forrest Jarrett, with his ostrich-skin boots and rattlesnake-banded Stetson. John was dressed unassumingly, in khakis and a short-sleeve plaid shirt. He had a short, neat haircut; reading glasses in his shirt pocket; and the slightly rounded build of a middle-aged man who still enjoyed dipping his corn bread in fresh milk. He didn't move slowly, but he seemed completely unhurried. He smiled and shook my hand, said hello, asked about the drive. I won't say John is quiet, because he's not, but he chooses his words carefully. He's the kind of older man—and by that I mean maybe sixty to my fifty—who is comfortable enough with himself to know that he doesn't need to say something just to fill the air, so most of the things he chooses to say are wise.

He gave me a leisurely tour of the property. The hand-crank corn grinder was in the first building up from the barn, the electric gristmill in the next. A larger garage held his tractor, and behind it, under the one tree on the hill, a huge craggy oak missing most of its limbs, was a collection of rusted metal pieces half buried in weeds. Now that I looked closely, I saw that half the hill was covered in old parts and pieces, but John didn't seem to care. He pointed out the pen for his two goats, an empty pen that usually held a pig, and at the top of the gravel road, two wooden chicken houses he had built himself. I had the impression that John, or one of his relatives before him, had built just about everything on the property.

Each building, I also noticed, featured a sign above the door explaining what it was for. The signs were wooden, with colorful bubble-shaped letters. John's wife was a teacher. The farm was set up for school tours. John liked to show the local children, many of whom no longer lived on working farms, what life was like a generation ago. He had also put up the signs for his special needs daughter, Lindsey. John's mother had named the farm Peaceful Valley to please her, and many of the signs said things like LINDSEY'S BARN or LINDSEY'S CHICKENS. Lindsey loved helping with the tours, he said, especially serving sandwiches and lemonade to the children in the barn.

"We held a wedding in here for my niece," John said matter-of-factly as he pushed open the new-looking barn doors. The barn, so shabby from the road, was beautiful inside. The farm was so slanted we had entered into the hayloft on the second floor, and the sunlight was flooding in slanting rays through the gaps in the slat-board sides, giving it a heavenly glow. It reminded me of a church, or the old tobacco barn at Angel-wood.

"Do you want to see the corn?"

We got in John's truck, crossed the road, and passed the jumbled sawmill. Inside, I could see the round six-foot rotor blade, with its two-inch teeth. The black dog from the house was running behind the truck.

"That dog follows me everywhere," John said, "but he's never once let me touch him."

We crossed Crooked Creek on a covered wooden bridge hidden from the road by a stand of maple trees John tapped for a small syrup-making operation. The creek was about ten feet wide; the cornfield was on the far side, hemmed in by trees. I had never seen corn so tall. When we pulled up, the stalks formed a solid wall.

"The ears take a long time to ripen," John said. "The stalks are so tall that a late summer storm can break them and destroy the crop. That's my main problem."

"What's your other problem?"

"Bears. Last summer, a mom and her cub came down to live on the edge of the woods. They probably ate half an acre between them."

"Why didn't you run them off?"

"I did, but they kept coming back." John shrugged. "I couldn't bring myself to hurt 'em."

We went back to the barn. John's daughter Lindsey, who

was in her early thirties, served us lemonade. John and I were, on the outside, a mismatched pair. I was elegantly and neatly dressed, with a barely contained energy. John was messy and sprawling, without any apparent desire to do anything more than what came naturally in the course of an afternoon. And yet I felt at home with John, even more than I had with Forrest. I liked him immediately, and his ramshackle farm had given me an idea.

"You have a lot of outbuildings, John," I said as Lindsey turned on country music, her favorite. "What about using one of them for distilling?"

John thought for a second, or maybe he was just watching the sunlight fall through the slats. He shook his head. "Nah," he said. "I don't want to get arrested."

He was right to be concerned. As long as moonshiners are making untaxed whiskey, the government is going to come after them. The saga of Popcorn Sutton had proved that.

"Oh, we won't get arrested, John," I said. "It's just a little experiment."

He wouldn't budge, but I'd heard him hesitate just a touch, and I could tell he wasn't truly opposed. So I took some Crooked Creek corn, called him a week later, and pushed some more. It took a few weeks of persuading, but I could tell he was coming around. John liked to think things through, but he had an entrepreneurial spirit just like my dad. He was restless to try new ideas. He already had half a dozen ventures going on at the farm; why not one more? Because it was against the law?

I drove back to the farm, on the pretense of buying more corn. "What if I applied for a permit," I said, "and we make it legal?"

I had no idea how hard getting legal would prove to be, but the most important thing in business and in life is to clear the obstacle directly in front of you before you worry about the ones down the road. And I knew I had cleared the last obstacle with John McEntire because of the way he smiled. I could tell he wanted to make a little mischief, more than he cared about making a little money.

"All right, Troy," he said. "Why don't we give it a try and see how it goes."

CHAPTER 18

PEACEFUL VALLEY

The summer of 2009 was my summer of whiskey. I brought my pressure cooker still to Peaceful Valley Farm the day after John agreed to lend me space (never delay, they might change their minds), and he and I cleared an old tilted shed for distilling. John was far handier than Charlie, I realized as he helped me set up my still, clamping the copper pipe to the pressure cooker and fixing the perfect angle for the copper condenser and its PVC cover.

I stepped back and looked at it. The operation was . . . shabby. It was very, very shabby. But I was in business.

I didn't have a plan. I had $20,000, and I knew I needed to create a great moonshine before the money ran out. I had an office in my house, and I put a giant Post-it note on the wall every time I thought of something I needed to do. Get place to distill. Check. Done. Get corn. Check. Water source? Yeast? Bottles for storing moonshine? Taste test? Market?

One step at a time, Troy. One obstacle at a time. That was my approach. It's not business school thinking, obviously, but it's entrepreneurship. Dad had taught me to be flexible, because Dad knew from experience you can never anticipate all the problems ahead. If I made a great moonshine, I had faith I could sell it. And honestly, right then, great moonshine was my focus.

I knew I had to be frugal, since I'd already spent $200 (1 percent of my total budget!) on a pressure cooker and copper pipes. So John and I went to a restaurant supply depot east of Asheville and dug through piles of mismatched items until we found two well-used restaurant-quality propane burners for $15 each, giving me a controllable heat source. John owned a hundred-gallon stainless steel pot and plastic barrel, so we had a mash cooker and fermentation chamber. So two days and $30 after John agreed to help me, I had a rudimentary distillery ready to start spiderlegging a few white squeezings.

All I needed was the mash. I started with a batch of whole-kernel Crooked Creek corn, stirring it in water from John's well and heating it at 180 degrees for exactly one hour. By then, the shed was so hot I could barely breathe. There were no fans, and the only ventilation was the air sneaking in between the wooden slats in the walls. It was eighty degrees and muggy, a typical North Carolina May afternoon, and the propane burners and boiling corn turned the place into a sauna. Long before I poured the mash into the fermentation barrel, I was sweating though my J.Crew shirt.

I left the mash in the barrel with cheesecloth over the top to keep out dust and critters. The wild yeast in the air would be attracted to the mash, and once those microscopic organisms started eating the corn sugars, their gaseous excretions would kick off the fermentation process. Now there was nothing to do but wait, so I headed home in the early afternoon to spend time with the boys.

I called John to check in the next day, but not much was happening. I called him the day after that, and every day for the next two weeks. Fermentation was taking place, but it was slow. Too slow. It took fifteen days before my mash was ready to distill.

That wasn't going to work.

I didn't realize it at the time, but the high fat content in Crooked Creek corn meant low sugar content. This would be great for the flavor of the whiskey and ideal for a smooth finish—when I got my method right. But it increased fermentation time, especially when using wild yeast.

I decided to try store-bought yeast for my next mash. But what kind? Fleischmann's from the grocery store, or more exotic varieties from wholesale distributors?

The answer was obvious: I needed to try them all. But it was also obvious that, at less than one batch of mash a week, it was going to take years to find the right recipe.

I talked it over with John, and we decided to ramp up production. I ordered more food-grade barrels and lined them up along one side of the building. In each one, I could ferment a different version of my mash, so that a batch would be ready to distill each morning. Some mashes used different yeasts; others used different grinding methods for John's corn. They had been cooked at different temperatures and for different lengths of time, left uncovered or tightly sealed, enhanced with different grain or left pure corn.

I knew I wanted to make corn liquor, because when they emigrated to the United States, the Scots-Irish had switched from barley to that New World grain. I'd learned that at the state archives in Raleigh, which I'd visited while waiting for

Forrest to decide I was trustworthy enough to distill with Jerry
Rogers. I made copies of everything the archivist could find on
moonshining in North Carolina—more than a thousand pages,
dating all the way back to the early 1800s—and studied them
during my free time at home. There were a lot of recipes, and
at first I was eager to try them all, but it didn't take me long to
realize recipes weren't going to be the secret to my success. A
good moonshine came down to two things: careful technique
and quality ingredients, especially the corn.

I liked the heirloom Crooked Creek corn. My gut told me
it was special. But I was a serious whiskey woman now, and
I wasn't going to simply assume it was the best option. So I
was determined to try every type of corn I could find, short of
Jerry Rogers's feed corn full of leaves and grass. Whole-kernel
yellow corn turned out to be the hardest to find in bulk, but
John tracked some down. John was resourceful. As I would
soon discover, he could get a good deal on just about anything.

I built my still in May and distilled my first batch of whiskey around the beginning of June. It was . . . anticlimactic. Just
a slow drip, like water from a leaky faucet. I watched for five
minutes, mesmerized, but you can only watch dripping for so
long. I had been working up to this moment for more than a
year. I'd been watching, talking, building, and planning. You'd
think that first batch would have been like giving birth, or at
least having a birthday. But I was too old to welcome birthdays
anymore, and I was far too practical to think I'd accomplished
anything by turning one barrel of mash into a quart of white
lightning. It was the first step of a long journey, not the last.

Still, I celebrated. I stuck my finger under the end of the
condenser pipe and tasted a drop of my very own moonshine.

Then John and I shared a spiderleg, straight from the jar.

It wasn't particularly good, but what did I expect? I didn't know what I was doing, and the first step is always a stumble.

But I was out the door. And that's what mattered.

At first I was distilling once a week, because of the long fermentation time. In hindsight, it was an ideal way to get comfortable being away from the boys, especially with Coulton's near-death experience still in my mind. By the time I had my seven mashes going at different fermentation stages, it was mid-June, and I was feeling comfortable with Coulton's health. By the second week of July, I was driving my ten-year-old white Mercedes to John's farm to distill a trial batch of white whiskey every day.

I should probably mention that white is my color. I love white. My house was white and decorated with a carved white cow skull. My car was white, inside and outside. I usually wore white blouses, along with my white earrings and a white pearl necklace, and my hair was white blond. I even kept a white fold-up table in my trunk, which I used as a portable work desk.

White, as you can imagine, is not ideal for distilling whiskey on a ramshackle farm. The sweat stained straight through my blouses, and no matter how careful I was, everything ended up covered with dust, dirt, oily gunk (from tinkering with my still), and spilled mash. At first I washed my car every couple of days, but it was utterly hopeless, so I stopped worrying. I was immaculate when I stepped out the door every morning at nine thirty, when the home health care professional arrived, but I accepted that I would be filthy by five thirty, when I arrived home at the end of her shift. It was like stepping out of my daily existence into a new life. By the time I'd made the thirty-minute drive to Peaceful Valley Farm, "mama" Troy was behind me, and "moonshine mama" Troy was ready to work.

And work it was. Physically difficult work, since I was stirring and cooking a new mash every morning to replace the one I distilled in the afternoon. And mentally difficult work, too. I wasn't just throwing things in a pot and boiling off the vapor; I was carefully making each batch, changing one factor each time to isolate the effect. I kept detailed notes: how hot, how long, how many ingredients and exactly how much of each. Did anything unexpected happen? How did each mash look? How clear was the liquor at the end? Some batches had an oily sheen. Some had a blue tint. The best batches looked like water.

How did it *smell*? A good moonshine cleared the nostrils, but it didn't burn them. It didn't smell acrid, like fingernail polish remover, or skunky and polluted. The smell was sharp, but the longer you inhaled, the more mellow and mouthwatering it became.

The most important factor, though, wasn't the look or smell. It was the taste. In the end, that's what mattered. And there is only one efficient way to measure the taste of a batch of moonshine: you drink it.

The good thing about moonshine is that you don't have to put it in a barrel and wait three years. My nine-foot-long copper-pipe condenser was open at the end, and the condensed liquor would drip out of it directly into a quart jar. I kept a piece of cheesecloth over the top to catch particulates and keep out gnats, but otherwise, the clear whiskey was almost ready the second it left the still. When a jar was half full, John and I would slide a new one in its place, add water to lower the alcohol content, and take a sip. Then we'd take another, because a bird can't fly on one wing. Then we'd discuss it, and I'd write down my notes. Then I'd tape a corresponding number to the jar, along with a few descriptive words (originally, things like "very good" or "weak," but later more specific ideas, like "woody" or "a little like horse manure"). Then I'd store that jar in the redbrick silo next to the barn. John had built dozens of shelves inside to store the maple syrup he made each fall. Before long, my jars had taken over most of the syrup space.

I realized through temperature experimentation that Alabama Clyde was distilling a bit too hot. And Jerry Rogers . . . Oh, Jerry Rogers. I don't think he was too interested in the taste of his moonshine, anyway. Jerry always bragged about the fact that his liquor was 160 proof, or 80 percent alcohol. I know now that a simple pot still is lucky to produce 140 proof, and that's in the hands of a serious distiller. But Jerry had his story, and he was sticking to it.

The thing that really complicated the tasting process, though, was that the moonshine in a distillation tasted vastly different depending on when in the run it was produced. The first 8 percent of a distillation is called the heads. (Some say as low as 2 percent, but I disagree.) The mash is heating up during this phase, so it's vaporizing the lighter alcohols that boil off at lower temperatures. The primary vapor in the heads is ethanol—yes, the gasoline additive—but it also contains a small percentage of acetone, methanol, aldehydes, and other impurities.

The last 25 percent of the distillation is the tails. At this point, the internal heat buildup raises the core temperature of the mash, boiling off the heaviest chemicals, like butanol and propanol. These are known as fusel alcohols. "Fusel" is the German word for "rotgut."

The middle 65–70 percent of the distillation, when the mash is cooking at the perfect temperature, is the heart. The heart is where the magic is. The liquor here is slightly sweet and deliciously smooth, because it contains almost no impurities. The heart is white whiskey, pure and true.

The mountain boys understood this phenomenon, even if they never called the separate parts of their distillations by those names. Alabama Clyde had alerted me to the different qualities in a run by telling me to always pour off the first five minutes of my distillation. Forrest had called his first pet 'n' pokes the "giveaways," meaning they came from either the beginning or the end of the run—the heads or the tails. The "keeper 'shine," as the old-timers like Forrest called the heart, was never sold, but kept for personal consumption or given to close friends. When Forrest came by my Asheville home to give me the good stuff, he was giving me the same moonshine. The difference was that, finally, he was giving me the heart.

In other words, *anyone* can make a decent moonshine, if you drink only the pure heart of the distillation. But major commercial distillers don't cut out the heart. They blend all three parts of the run together, so that what you are drinking is heads + heart + tails.

They'll tell you the tails add flavor. I suppose they do, in the same way adding a dirty dish towel to clean water changes the whole bucket. The aldehydes and acetones in the heads are poisons; they give whiskey its distinctive burn and bite. They also give you a headache.

Aficionados think of this burn and bite as essential to the whiskey-drinking experience. Whiskey should be harsh, they say. It should tear into your throat. It should put a fire in your stomach. You should feel it the next day. In this tradition, great whiskey is created by manipulating the bite.

Fair enough. Flavor is the essence of whiskey. But there are other ways to get great flavor, like using the right corn or grain.

The real reason commercial bourbons, scotches, and whiskeys are full of heads and tails isn't to create flavor. It's because commercial distillers can't separate them. The big companies don't use pot stills. They use continuous distillation columns where new mash is added at intervals to never-ending runs, so everything mixes together before it hits the storage barrels. Only single-batch distilleries that fill their stills every morning and run a mash from start to finish can separate the heart.

But not all single-batch distilleries bottle the pure heart, even though they can, and the reason is obvious. I've seen commercials where distillers brag about their dedication to quality by saying they give up the "angel's share," the part of the whiskey that evaporates during aging. That's 1 percent of the run! I must have been giving up the "angel's choir," because bottling only the heart means throwing away up to 30 percent of the distillation. From a business standpoint, that's madness.

And yet, I was determined to do exactly that. I didn't want to use poison to flavor my moonshine. I wanted a product that was smooth, delicious, and easy to drink. I was creating a brand, and I was pretty clear about what I wanted that brand to be: the world's highest-quality heirloom whiskeys. My operation was going to be pure heart, in every way, from the business practices to the corn. To this day, every drop of liquor I bottle comes from the heart. Guaranteed.

Of course, that meant I had to *find* the heart of each distillation. We do that now by smell. The heads smell like fingernail polish remover. The tails smell like dirty socks. The heart smells like whiskey. The difference is distinct. With a bit of training and a diligent approach to distilling, the edges of the heart are easy to find.

John and I didn't know that back then, though. We were going by taste. So we'd be sipping at different points in the run, trying to find the heart. The first few sips would be thin and abrasive. The last few would be dirty and rough. But boy, when we nailed it, we'd know. I'd take a sip and it would slide down my throat, leaving a sweet corn aftertaste in my mouth.

I'd look at John, and he'd be smiling. "That's it, Troy," he'd say. "That right there is the pure heart."

CHAPTER 19

THE THUMPER

I kept my promise to John McEntire and sent away to the United States government for the requirements to become a legal distiller. A manual arrived six weeks later. It was three hundred pages long.

I lugged the manual around for months, trying to make sense of it. I read it on my little fold-out white table during my breaks between cooking mash and distilling, and I read it in bed at night. I asked advice from John McEntire, a man who could probably build a working tractor out of toothpicks, and he couldn't make anything out of it, either. I called the TTB (Alcohol and Tobacco Tax and Trade Bureau) and was put through to Lang Guenther, the official who processed permits for my region.

His advice helped. Barely. There were so many rules for sites, equipment, supplies, inventory, warehousing, waste, fire, health, security, marketing . . . It was so overwhelming that,

basically, I called Lang for advice on every step. After a few
weeks, I was spending as much time trying to figure out how
to get legal as I was cooking whiskey.

The first thing I figured out was that John's shed wasn't
up to code. There must have been a hundred rules about the
distilling building, and I think the shed failed all of them. The
place didn't even have electricity, unless you counted the exten-
sion cord. So about a month into the process, I went to Mar-
ion, North Carolina, and bought a building.

Actually, it was just an eighteen-by-twenty-one-foot backyard storage shed delivered off the back lot of the local hard-
ware store, but it was the biggest single purchase for my
business that entire year. It was like a small barn, red with
white trim and two fancy roll-up doors, one in the front and
one in the back. John built a level gravel pad and installed
it halfway up his hill of mismatched sheds, across from the
chicken coop and lamb pen. I'd be giving the shed to him as
payment when I left, so it was nice to know he'd have at least
one level building.

It took us a few days to move everything in and set it up,
but when we did, the new "distillery" seemed like paradise.
There was a ventilation fan (thank you, electricity!), and the
big doors allowed us to control the airflow and temperature,
not to mention the cleanliness. In the old shed, I'd had to cover
everything when John was grinding corn, because the breeze
would bring corn dust through the slats in the walls.

I had other practical matters to attend to as well. I had to
adhere to the fire code, so the burners and heaters needed to be
situated correctly. I had to inventory every night and invest in
special locks for the doors. Whiskey is a valuable commodity,
and one that naturally attracts the interest of ne'er-do-wells.
The Alcohol and Tobacco Tax and Trade Bureau (emphasis on

tax!) wanted to make sure no product was misappropriated into the gullets of local inebriates before the government got its slice.

At least the disposal of mash proved easy, since we were in hog country. A local farmer took the mash off my hands to use as feed. Not only was it a free exchange, but once the hogs were fattened on Crooked Creek corn, the farmer offered to give me one to butcher.

"That's what the tree's for," John said, motioning to the lone oak behind the shed. The family had strung a hog from its branches every winter for as long as he could remember.

Now that I was appropriately situated (I hoped), I needed to make my distilling process more professional. If this was going to be a business, it had to be more sustainable than the hobby processes of Jerry Rogers or Alabama Clyde. My first goal was to simplify the mash-cooking process. It took an hour of constant stirring to make mash, and that was hard labor. My shoulders were sore every night. John helped, but even with the two of us, stirring fifty gallons of an oatmeal-thick substance was a grind. We needed a mechanical solution, but I couldn't afford the kind of industrial mixers they use in commercial distilleries.

John suggested boat propellers. He had a friend with two old outboard motors that were never going to work, and he was pretty sure the man would give him the props. I had figured out by this time that John was active in the local barter culture. The stuff lying around on his hillside was junk, but it wasn't worthless. Middle-aged country types would come by and take pieces every now and then, and John would travel to their properties and take things he needed. They must have had photographic memories, because they always seemed to know exactly what they wanted and exactly where it was in the knee-high grass. And like John, they must have had a genius for figuring out how to use old parts, like boat propellers off dead motors, in ways they had never been designed for.

The next day, John rigged the boat propellers to a long handle so that we could raise them in and out of the mash, flipped an electrical switch, and lo and behold, we had a mechanized mash-stirring system, all for about $15.

The good times lasted for two minutes, until the propellers started to vibrate. After another minute, they were rattling so violently they probably would have knocked down our original wooden shed. I turned them off. John and I tinkered with the setup. It was no use. The propellers weren't balanced. We couldn't stop the banging.

"We're going to have to shave down the blades," John said.

Charlie came out and helped us shape the blades. By now he could tell I was serious about my moonshine, and I think he wanted to check out Pleasant Valley Farm. I'm sure he was impressed by my portable backyard shed, especially after spending two years building eight houses and a million-dollar community center at Whisper Mountain.

"Now we need to increase production capacity," I said once the blades were working correctly.

Charlie just shook his head at my ambition. Poor man. John McEntire said, "We need to talk with Benny."

Benny was John's old friend and trading partner. He was sort of a cross between John and Forrest Jarrett, a low-key farmer who had a knack for telling stories. I've never been sure if John McEntire made moonshine when he was younger. Whenever I ask him, he always hesitates, then just smiles and says, "Well . . . nah."

Benny's father, on the other hand, had been a well-known local moonshiner, and Benny wasn't hiding it. He loved it. He'd settle into a folding chair with a jar of our pure heart in his hand and tell stories about his father's old liquor still, which was on up the Crooked Creek valley, on the backside of a hill.

"You had to walk through a tall grass field to get to the still, and that field was full of rattlesnakes," Benny said. "My dad strapped old metal gutters to his legs. The rattlesnakes would strike it so often it sounded like hail on a tin roof. Bam. Bam. Bam, in the middle of the night. Nobody but Daddy ever bothered that still."

"Is that true?" I asked John once Benny had left.

"Well . . . nah," he said. "Benny's just telling tales. Everyone knows his daddy's still was underneath their front porch."

Many days that fall, as the weather turned colder, John, Benny, and I sat on folding chairs at Peaceful Valley Farm, swapping stories while the white lightning dripped and the mash fermented, seven recipes in a row. The long grass browned up like hay, and the leaves on the trees down by Crooked Creek turned golden red. The black dog lay in the sunlight a few feet away or hopped up to follow when I checked on the still. Very occasionally, a car would pass on the two-lane road, but if they ever looked our way, all they saw was two older gentlemen and what appeared to be their blond real estate agent, sipping whiskey and shooting the breeze.

Actually, I was probably sipping lemonade, especially when Lindsey was with us, or the boys were out for a visit on those long glorious Indian summer days. I had a palate for moonshine by then; I could taste the difference between strains of corn. But I wasn't a drinker. A spiderleg or two, and I'd had enough. It was the ritual that inspired me, not the alcohol. The steady drip of a perfect distillation. The slow bubbling of the fermenting mash. The smell of the shed, like an old Irish pub on the fourth rainy day in a row. Talking on a rural hillside while passing a jar. It felt like something that had been going on for a hundred years, and I loved it.

After a while, John's neighbor figured out what was going on and started coming over to sample our product, too. I wasn't worried. The neighbor was John's older brother, a retired doctor, and he had a great palate for white whiskey. I put his comments in my notebook for future reference, just as I always had my own.

"You should try distilling in whiskey barrels," Benny said, about the time I had forgotten that he was supposed to be giving me advice on traditional distilling methods. "That's the way my daddy did it."

The method, as Benny explained it, used three standard wooden barrels and a converted dairy tank, where the water was heated. The steam was piped into the first barrel, known as the cooking barrel, to heat the mash. When the mash was hot enough, the vapor would travel though a stainless steel pipe to the thumper barrel, which gathered it and acted as a reflux chamber. When the second barrel was full, the hot mash vapor was piped to the third barrel, where the whiskey condensed inside a fifty-inch copper coil submerged in cold water. The result was a smooth whiskey with a light brown tint and a slight smoky flavor imparted from the wood of the second barrel. Benny's old man had bought his barrels from the general store in Old Fort, where they held flour and corn. I purchased mine from Woodford Reserve, where in their former life they were used to age one of Kentucky's finest bourbons.

Honestly, my base mash distilled in a wooden barrel may be my favorite unaged whiskey, because the barrels balance the hints of sweet corn in my moonshine with a nice oak finish. If I could distill that way on a large scale, I probably would. That 'shine has *character*. But I'd have to line up three hundred barrels to fulfill demand, and the taste would differ noticeably from batch to batch, something customers generally frown on. And, sadly, the barrel system probably wouldn't be up to the massive United States distilling code.

At Peaceful Valley Farm, though, the barrel still was a big step forward. It was my first large distillation, using a truly traditional method. And it was the first still John McEntire and I built together from scratch. I went to Lowe's to buy the coiled copper the vapor would condense on inside the barrels, and the checkout clerk joked, "You're not building a still, are you?"

I thought about the old stick who had shaken his head at me the first time I bought copper piping and thought, *Twice! What is going on with this Lowe's?* I guess moonshine was more entrenched in the mountains than I realized.

It was late on a Saturday when we finally finished building the still. On Sunday morning, John woke up early to get the fire going under the dairy tank. He had woken up at sunrise every day of his life, so he'd taken to starting the process, since a distillation took about eight hours.

After making sure all was in order, John went back to his house. Knowing him, he probably did a hundred other chores around the farm. About nine, he heard explosions coming from our shed. He rushed—no, wait, John McEntire never rushes. He walked casually down to the "distillery" and rolled up the back door. The thumper barrel was popping like a cannon and shaking like a dog. John stood in the doorway and stared at the barrel. "Well, law," he probably said. He wasn't worried. It was just the vapor building up inside. They called it the thumper barrel for a reason.

John turned, finally, and looked off down the road. The church his family had attended for seven generations was around the next bend, just out of sight. It was close enough

that John and his wife could often hear the congregation singing, so he knew they could hear our moonshine thumping.

The thought made him smile. He was still smiling when he
told me about it the next day. "When I was a boy, there were
men in that church on a Sunday morning," he said, "sitting up
straight and nodding along to the sermon, who I knew had
been at their stills until the sun come up. The preacher always
preached against the evils of liquor, that was his cause, and
those men never batted an eye. Nobody did."

John had no problem with the religion or the moonshiners.
He just found such hypocrisy amusing.

"I can promise you," he told me with a gleam in his eye,
"that there were at least twelve men in that church yesterday
morning who knew exactly what they were hearing. And all
twelve of them wished they were up here cooking with me."

CHAPTER 20

A PLACE OF MY OWN

They slaughtered the hog that had been fattened on Crooked Creek moonshine mash about two weeks before Christmas, in the freezing final days of 2009. John McEntire strung the carcass up in the barren tree behind the distilling shed, as the McEntire family had for generations, so the blood could drain away. My friend Dwayne, a retired butcher, carved it into pieces, his breath blowing like smoke in the freezing air. John seasoned and preserved the meat as it came down off the hog, then stored it in the smokehouse. The cold would preserve the salted pork for the next two months, as it had before refrigeration came to this valley fifty years ago.

The winter kept me frozen too, for the most part. The new shed had been passable in the summer, but it was brutally cold in January and February. I bought insulation, and John found a local kid to install it on every inch of the walls and ceiling. The exposed side of the insulation was silver; it looked like we were working inside a Mylar balloon, or in an airtight outpost on the surface of Mars. I bought a few space heaters, and when the mash was cooking, the room could get toasty. But mostly, it was cold. In the summer and fall, I had set up my worktable outside, in the fresh air. Around November, I moved the table inside the shed. By December, I was doing most of my paper-work in my car, with the heater on full blast.

Early morning was inconvenient. I usually couldn't feel my fingers and toes for the first hour. Night was an actual problem. There's a reason "moonshine season" has traditionally ended in the fall, and it isn't only because sitting in the woods in January isn't much fun. Cold can kill yeast. I ran space heaters round the clock, but the temperature inside the shed still dropped almost to freezing overnight, affecting the fermenting mash. Some mornings, the bubbling of fermentation would be almost stopped, and even if I got it going full bore again, the interruption changed the characteristics of the finished prod-uct. I couldn't cook good whiskey in these conditions, because I couldn't raise the internal temperature of the mash high enough on ten-degree nights.

John and I were stumped, so I did what I always did: I called an expert. In this case, the expert was a guy who called himself Colonel Wilson. Benny's barrel still had been an experiment. I had always known I'd need an actual pot still to make great moonshine, and my search had led me to Colonel Wilson, who hand-built traditional copper stills in the Ozark Mountains of Arkansas. There was a six-month wait for my order, but I fig-ured since the Colonel had my deposit, I was already a client. And if he was an experienced moonshiner, he might know how to keep mash warm on a cold winter night.

Colonel Wilson suggested aquarium heaters. Yep, you heard that right, simple aquarium heaters, like kids have in their bedroom fish tanks. They were designed to maintain an exact temperature underwater, since some fish are sensitive to changes in their environment. The heaters would work just as well in mash, the Colonel assured me. I could even use more than one per mash barrel, if the outside temperature got too cold. He was right. It took three in each mash barrel (the pet store employee thought I was nuts when I bought twenty-five heaters), but the next morning, my yeasts were digesting away.

Most of my work that winter, though, didn't involve making moonshine. I was starting a business, not just distilling. When I had started planning in my home office, I had a full wall of Post-its labeled "product development" containing all the steps to make a great moonshine. Now I had the other three walls covered with Post-it notes, too. The second wall was "licensing and code." I'd been working on that since the fall, but I still had a hundred pages left to get through the licensing manual. The third wall was "business structure." The fourth was "funding and sales." That's where I would start making money. But to get to that final wall, I needed to get through the other three first.

I suppose I could have kept it simple. I could have stayed in the shed at Peaceful Valley Farm. Once I got my distilling license, it would have been legal for me to sell whatever I distilled on John McEntire's farm. Considering that I was spending hundreds of hours and thousands of dollars trying to get my operation up to code, that might have been the smartest option.

But I didn't want to run a business from a country shack. I wanted to found a real distillery, and that meant marketing, selling, and displaying my moonshine to the highest possible standards. So it was time to tackle my third wall: business development.

As always, the first thing I did when presented with the problem was figure out the best person to ask for help. If you were starting a business in Asheville, North Carolina, that person was Pat Whalen, the man behind Julian Price's efforts to revitalize downtown in the 1990s. After Price's death in 2001, Pat had continued to support local entrepreneurs through Public Interest Projects (PIP), the business development group he and Price had founded. Dozens of businesses in downtown Asheville owed not only their founding but their continued success to Pat Whalen's mentorship. He had dedicated twenty years of his life to the small business owners of Asheville.

By the time I started distilling at Peaceful Valley Farm, though, Pat was primarily focused on his own development projects. Between PIP and other private ventures, there were more square feet of new development planned for downtown Asheville than had existed in 1989. Plus, Pat was part owner of the Orange Peel, a legendary independent music venue on the south side of downtown that had opened in 2002. Pat was still helping the people he'd worked with in the past, but for the most part, he wasn't taking on new entrepreneurs.

Fortunately, I knew his wife, Karen Ramshaw.

The entrepreneurial community in Asheville is relatively small, and it's incestuous in the best ways. In Austin, the family roots went back generations, and outsiders were often unwelcome. After a few years, I'd mostly stayed clear, focusing instead on raising the boys. In Asheville, the roots didn't go nearly as deep. There was a small group of old-money families that had hung on since the glory days of the 1920s, but most of the successful people in town had been there for only a generation, and many—like Julian Price, Charlie and Rebecca from Tomato Jam, Oscar Wong from Highland Brewing Company, and the ambitious young chefs opening restaurants downtown—had grown up elsewhere and arrived in the last twenty years. They welcomed outsiders like me, and they accommodated Marshall and Coulton, too.

I met Karen Ramshaw at a school ballet recital for my neighbor's daughter. Luke was playing football and lacrosse, and I made many friends at his games and practices. That was the Asheville social scene: low-key get-togethers, often centered on our children's activities. Nobody cared about being hip, and nobody really worried about getting rich. The town was friendly enough to make a place for a mother with two special needs children, and small enough that when you went to the grocery store, you'd probably run into someone you knew.

Once I became serious about moonshine, I worked to turn my friends into contacts who could help my business. Luck is the result of connections, right? That may sound impersonal or opportunistic, but it's not. You can be friends with someone because you genuinely like them and also ask for their help. Everyone who is successful does this, which isn't to say it's easy. Asking for help, whether from friends or experts, is hard. Fear of asking holds many people back. The key is to value the friendship, no matter their answer, and always be willing to provide if a friend reaches out to you in return.

Karen Ramshaw was a good friend. We didn't see each other much, since I was so busy with work and family, but we liked each other. She was interested in my life and loving toward the boys. I thought our friendship meant that when I went looking for a local business mentor, I was set. There was no way Pat Whalen could refuse to help me.

I was wrong.

"I'm sorry, Troy," he said brusquely. Pat was a lawyer and a numbers guy. He wasn't the touchy-feely type. "I've got more than I can handle right now."

Sorry, Pat, I thought, *but I'm not taking no.*

"Asheville has so many breweries that it's nicknamed Beer Town, USA. But it doesn't have a distillery. Asheville needs a distillery."

"You're probably right. I don't have the time."

"Moonshine is from the mountains. It's our heritage."

"It's not possible, Troy. I'm sorry."

All through the winter, I was working on Pat. I kept calling and calling, and he kept saying no. That speaks to an addendum I need to add to Dad's fundamental belief that no just means the other person doesn't have enough information yet: The other person will always say no the first time. *Always.* And they will always say no the second time. And probably a bunch of times after that, too. The important thing is to keep trying. Often, the fact that you are so passionate that you will never give up is the missing piece of information they need.

It didn't work on Pat. He and Karen went away to their second home in Mexico, and I sat in my distilling shed, in the freezing cold, shadowed by the memory of the slaughtered hog outside my door. I thought about the road ahead. It had been two years since Forrest Jarrett introduced me to the keeper 'shine. I'd busted my hump, and all I had to show for it was a small shed, a beautiful but impractical whiskey-barrel still, and one damn fine recipe for moonshine.

Was the sacrifice worth it? Could I really pull this off?

My moonshine obsession had taken me away from my family, although I hadn't abandoned them by any means. I still spent time each week with Marshall at his alphabet board, recording everything he wrote. I was still up in the middle of the night, soothing Coulton. I still went to Luke's high school sporting events—or at least the ones in Asheville, since traveling to away games was tough. I took the boys to Whisper

Mountain whenever I had free time, because I still loved Whisper Mountain: the tranquility there, the feeling of being away. I was on the website as a partner, and I took that seriously. When a national truffle convention fell through at the Biltmore Estate, I invited them to use our community lodge. It didn't have overnight rooms, but it had a large patio, a fireplace, and gorgeous mountain views. I even wrangled a write-up in *Southern Living*. Work was slow in the winter, but I put on my work gloves every week, usually on Sundays, my day off from moonshine, and did whatever Charlie needed me to do.

But in my heart, I had pulled away. My entrepreneurial energy was at Peaceful Valley Farm, not Whisper Mountain. I had spent hundreds of hours in my distilling shed with John, studying my notes or monitoring temperatures and cooking times. Sometimes Charlie would come out to help me with a particularly thorny issue. In warmer weather, I had brought the boys to have lemonade with Lindsey and see the chickens. They came for John McEntire's syrup-making weekend, and even for his annual family reunion in the barn. Marshall loved it. He wanted to *feel* this place his mother went away to every day. But Coulton didn't like Peaceful Valley. There were no paved paths for his wheelchair, and the farm was messy and loud.

This was my place, I realized, not Coulton's, not Charlie's or Luke's, not Marshall's. This small shack, with its silver insulation and bubbling mash, was the proverbial "room of one's own," as Virginia Woolf put it. The private space every woman needs to pursue her dreams. It had taken me fifty years to find it, and there was no way I was going to give it up.

I called Pat Whalen the day I heard he was back from Mexico. I begged for his help. I don't think he expected that; I think my persistence finally convinced him. With a sigh, he invited

me to his office in the basement of a public assistance apartment building he had rehabbed in downtown Asheville in the
late 1990s.

"Troy," he said, "starting a small business means running
through walls. Are you ready to do that?"

I might have laughed. I'd been running through walls my
whole life. I'd run through a wall of nos just to get this meeting.

"I'm ready," I told him. "Don't worry about me. I'll do
whatever I have to do."

"Okay then," he said, "I have a deal for you. I will charge
you one dollar, and provide three hours of advice and men-
toring each week. If, at the end of a year, I haven't earned that
dollar, I will refund fifty percent of my fee."

"All right," I said. "It's a steep price, but if you're willing to
take half the risk, I think I can handle the other half."

"Good," he said. "Now, let's see your business plan."

Business plan?

Business plan! What the . . . ?

I'd watched Dad start six or seven businesses. I'd started
a few businesses myself. Neither Dad nor I had ever created
what would be called a business plan. We were *entrepreneurs*.
Entrepreneurs understood that plans were useless, because
everything changed every day. Entrepreneurship wasn't about
sticking to a path. It was about being reactive and quick on
your feet, taking advantage of whatever the day threw at you,
and avoiding new dangers at every turn. A business couldn't
anticipate the purchase of twenty-five aquarium heaters. It
never would have approved of the making of a whiskey-barrel
still. A business plan was nothing but a lead weight, tying you
down. I couldn't believe that Pat Whalen, an entrepreneurial
legend in Asheville, was asking me about something as mun-
dane as a business plan.

"I'm sorry, Pat. I don't have a written plan. It's all in my head."

Pat stared at me. "I thought you were serious about this, Troy."

"I am serious, Pat."

"Not if you don't have a business plan."

"Well . . ."

"Do you have an accountant?"

"No."

"Do you know anything about accounting?"

"I used to do bookkeeping . . . twenty years ago."

"Do you have a budget?"

I didn't even bother to answer.

"Do you know where your expenses are going?"

Yes, to the next daily emergency.

"Do you know your business niche? Your competition? Have you researched real estate? How long until your product can get to market? How much will it cost to get it there?"

I started to break down. That's not the way I am, and I didn't expect it. I was listening to Pat belittle everything I'd done and suddenly I was getting emotional and then I was saying something that must have been in the back of my mind for a long time.

"I'm alone."

Pat stopped.

"I've done it all. The paperwork. The distilling. The planning. The sourcing and buying of supplies. The business development. I started with nothing. With no one." And that's when I started to cry. "Even my husband," I said, "doesn't understand."

I stopped, because as a businesswoman crying was the last thing I could allow myself to do. I pulled myself back together.

"I'm alone, Pat," I said, "with no backing and no experience. But look how far I've come."

Pat wasn't moved. He's not the sort to be impressed with sentimentality. Success is hard; get used to the struggle. He handed me information on writing a business plan, along with a few good samples. "Come back when you're finished," he said.

I got up to leave. I must have looked frustrated, because Pat reached out his hand. "Don't worry, Troy," he said. "It's only the first day. We have a long way to go before I earn that dollar."

CHAPTER 21

PARTNER

Of course, I wasn't alone. I was on my own with paperwork, inspections, distillery space, equipment purchases, sales, business planning, marketing ideas, budgeting, and accounting. But in my whiskey making at Peaceful Valley Farm, I had a partner. John McEntire.

We were, by accident or luck or fate, a perfect match. I was energetic, ambitious, and restless. I drove eighty miles an hour to Peaceful Valley Farm, tailgating most of the way, and always arrived in a cloud of dust with two or three new ideas. John was calm, practical, and methodical. No matter how eager I was to let fly with an inspiration (some solid, some half-baked, some barely baked at all), John just nodded, then casually took the idea apart to see if it was possible.

Did I mention that he was a trained chemist? He had a degree from Appalachian State, a well-respected North Carolina state university a few hours away in the mountain town of

Boone. Before becoming a teacher, he had worked as a scientist for a lumber company. He had an analytic mind and the ability to break experiments down into their component parts.

And like any good chemist, he knew the value of precision. I had started off, like my mentors in the mountains, estimating the right temperature, cooking time, and amount of fermentation in the mash by look, feel, and smell. As I'd gone along, I'd learned from studying books and archives that while distilling is an art, it's also a science. Every still had exact temperatures, times, and pressures that would produce the best whiskey. Finding those points meant monitoring not only the finished product but the process as well. The first day I brought in an instrument to test the alcohol content of my moonshine, John said, "See you got a hydrometer. Used to use those in my lab."

"Well, what else did you use?"

Before long, I had a brick gauge (not actually a brick, more like a syringe) to measure the fermentation of my mash and high-tech thermometers to measure internal temperatures. I tested my mash alkalinity with high-quality pH strips. I began to measure and chart my vaporizing temperature to a tenth of a degree. The details put the devil in the whiskey, after all. If the mash was one degree too hot when it vaporized, or a slight bit too acidic when I added it to the still, I could taste the difference.

I decided to try filtering my moonshine. The best way to filter liquor is to run it through charcoal as soon as it's distilled. I started out running it through a Brita filter, like the kind your refrigerator uses to clean the tap water. When I mentioned trying something better, John nodded, as always. By that afternoon, he had built a large filter out of scrounged PVC pipe and a mesh screen. The next day, I filled the homemade filter box with store-bought charcoal and ran my moonshine through it.

I switched the type and brand of charcoal every day for two weeks, waiting for the magic to happen. No magic. Didn't matter if it was Kingsford or Fogo 100% Natural, I couldn't taste any difference in my moonshine.

"We need to make our own charcoal," I said.

John smiled. "Well, my brother up in Raleigh makes medical-grade charcoal. I suspect he can give us some tips."

"Give him a call," I said.

When I arrived the next morning, John and his brother were standing over a fire, seasoning oak chips on a rack. It was a cold spring morning, and frost lingers into April in the high hills of North Carolina. The fire felt nice. But the oak chips didn't do much for the whiskey. So we tried maple, apple, and a few others. John's brother showed him how to build a better box to heat the wood, and how to jury-rig a tight screen so the moonshine would drain more slowly and filter longer.

After few weeks, we settled on cherry. The cherry wood gave the whiskey a slight richness to cut the sweetness, and the filtered liquor was smooth.

John was like that: part scientist, part tinkerer, slow operator. Weather permitting, he always wore a short-sleeve button-down shirt with his reading glasses in the pocket like a chemist, but he rolled his syllables like an old Southern farmer. He told me, "When I went up to Appalachian for college, I had to take an English course. The first day, the professor handed out a list of old mountain phrases that were disappearing from the language. I looked at that list and thought, *Well, law, I use every one of these.*"

The best example of John's unique genius was the steel tank. I had perfected my mash, cooking it to 180 degrees for one hour, with the boat propeller stirring at a set speed. I had a thermometer, pH strips, and the brick gauge, and when everything was perfect, I'd turn off the burner. But the process was still flawed, because the mash took too long to cool. I was over-cooking it slightly, in the same way you overcook a perfect hard-boiled egg if you don't put it in icy water when it's done.

I couldn't add icy water to the mash. That would change the consistency. I couldn't rely on the outside temperature, which fluctuated from day to day. So after much discussion, John sug-gested a two-layer steel "jacket" tank to put around the mash cooker. As soon as we turned off the heat, we'd fill the one-inch gap between the steel layers of the jacket tank with cold water. This would rapidly cool the mash without touching it. Don't ask me why the tank had to be steel. John's chemistry training told him steel was the best way to control the temperature, and I trusted his opinion.

Steel tanks, though, are expensive, and I was short on cash. So Charlie drew the engineering plans, and John found a local welder who could fabricate it. The steel cost $500, and the welding fee was another $500. A thousand dollars was most of the rest of my money, but I knew I had to invest everything I had to get every detail right. No cutting corners. Otherwise, what was the point?

The welder was good. The tank was exactly what I'd asked for. If he had stopped with the fabrication, everything would have been fine. But before delivering it, he decided to pump the tank full of pressurized air to check for leaks. There were no leaks. So the pressure built up and, eventually, the inside layer of the tank crumpled so badly that it was impossible to fix. He brought the tank to my shed anyway. It was unusable.

He wasn't deterred. He'd made the tank. He wanted to be paid. I suggested he get more steel and try again. This time he could actually make what I'd hired him for. He refused.

"I'm not going to pay it," I snapped when I received the

bill. I was down to my last dollars, I was neck-deep in business plans, and I didn't plan on paying for something I couldn't use.

Besides, it's important in business to stand your ground, especially as a woman. Men always assume, until you prove otherwise, that they can run you down.

John let me get all worked up before speaking. "You can do that if you want, Troy," he said when I'd worn myself out, "but not if we want to keep peace with the neighbors."

I sighed. John was right. I shouldn't be stubborn. I needed the community on my side. I paid the welder $500 to cover the cost of the steel. I thought that was more than fair.

A few weeks later, John got an angry call from his uncle Leroy. "What's this I hear about you not paying your debts?" Leroy barked.

Leroy was in his nineties and lived four miles away, on a little farm he'd owned and operated most of his life. Leroy may have been elderly, but he hadn't lost his fire. The year before, he'd been caught going seventy-five miles per hour through Old Fort, where the speed limit was twenty-five. John had gotten the phone call from the sheriff. "Now, John, we all know Leroy, and we all love him. What are we going to do about this driving situation?"

John talked to Leroy and convinced him to give up his driver's license. It was long past time for that to happen, and everyone in the area knew it, especially the relieved sheriff, who dropped the speeding charges.

Now word had gotten back to Leroy that the welder was talking all over, saying he'd done work for John McEntire and hadn't been paid. Leroy was in no mood to let his nephew ruin the family's reputation.

John told him what had happened. "She still paid him for the steel," John said. "She didn't have to do that, Uncle Leroy."

"I'll take care of it," Leroy snapped.

Rumor has it Leroy caught up to the welder a few days later and straightened him out. The bad-mouthing stopped. John and I figured out how to use the collapsed tank, since I couldn't afford another. After a couple weeks of banging on it, we got it working, but it was not very professional looking and hard as heck to clean.

The moral of the story, I suppose, is it would have been impossible for me to distill such a high-quality heirloom moonshine without John McEntire's expertise, ingenuity, and calming influence—not to mention his Crooked Creek corn.

Of course, it would have been impossible for John to create that moonshine without my ambition, energy, and constant pushing for a better option.

And if he'd distilled a good moonshine, John was far too laid-back and hands-off to have ever been able to sell it. In fact, he never would have bothered to try.

And if he had tried, he never would have succeeded in getting a license, because John had one major flaw that drove me absolutely nuts: he was messy.

That junk-strewn hillside was like a window into his soul. John couldn't for the life of him be bothered to put anything in its proper place. He'd throw instruments on a dirty table and leave spills on the ground. The man was a trained chemist, and yet he always "forgot" to clean his instruments. If I was gone for a few days, caring for the boys or working on the business, that mess on the hillside would have somehow made its way into the shed. For every day away, I figured it was two extra hours of cleaning up.

"Throw that away, John," I'd say whenever he had an old pipe or fitting we didn't need.

"Naw," he'd say. "It might come in handy one day."

Sure, much of that junk came in handy, but it was killing us, too. We had to pass health codes, fire codes, waste-disposal codes . . . we had codes for our codes. Leaving filthy instruments and rusted metal lying around was unacceptable. I came in every morning and cleaned the shop, first thing, especially after the last piece of the operation was finally delivered: the professional copper pot still built by Colonel Wilson in the Ozark Mountains.

Well, "professional" might not be the right word. It passed federal code—I checked that with my contact Lang Guenther at the TTB—but "practical" and "high-quality" are probably better adjectives, since Colonel Wilson didn't seem concerned with things like rules. For one thing, his "colonel" outfit made him look more like Colonel Sanders than a veteran. And for another, he provided a link on his website for a free moonshine/alcohol permit. When you clicked through the link, though, it clearly stated that the ethanol license was for the creation of fuel only. He also had a section on avoiding taxes, traffic tickets, and other assorted forms of "tyranny" by becoming a sovereign citizen. The plan involved putting 000-00-0000 as your social security number on a United States passport application, among other things. I had a feeling that wouldn't work. But it felt authentic. Colonel Wilson was cut from the same cloth as his moonshining forefathers.

And his blue mountain still was a work of art, handcrafted from high-quality copper for even heat distribution, with a built-in temperature gauge and a hydrometer to measure proof. (Measuring proof is required by law, because the manufacturer is taxed on the amount of alcohol produced, not the amount of liquid. Eighty proof, for instance, means your liquor is 40 percent alcohol, so you are taxed on 40 percent of your liquid volume.) The Colonel's heritage design, popularized in the Ozark Mountains more than a hundred years ago, included a vertical chamber that he told me to pack with steel wool to increase the surface area for condensing. While that advice seemed dubious, at best, the still was beautiful, tall and thin with an almost feminine shape. When John and I set it up in the shed, you could see the sassy curve of its hips. It was a perfect fit for this whiskey mama.

It took us a few months of experimenting and adjusting to learn how to use the new still. The first couple runs, in fact, came out blue. That turned out to be oxidation from the copper, as Colonel Wilson explained on the phone. I have to say, Colonel Wilson turned out to be a gem of a guy. He always took the time to talk John and me through any problems, even if we didn't always take his advice.

By the summer of 2010, we were ready for our final inspection. We had mastered our code-approved still. We had passed all the county and state requirements for a food-related business, like fire, sanitation, health, and zoning. It was funny to see the code enforcers' faces when they realized they had driven twenty miles to inspect a small shed bought off the back lot of a portable-building wholesaler.

Now all I needed to apply for my federal license was the state's approval of our shed as an "alcohol manufacturing facility." The license would allow me to legally distill whiskey. It wouldn't allow me to sell it. I would still have to get government bottling and labeling approval, and I hadn't even begun that journey. But it would be an accomplishment nonetheless. I'd be a legal moonshiner at last.

I thought I'd fail the inspection at least once, because, you know . . . that manual of rules . . . all three hundred pages of them. How could I possibly get everything right? But when the state inspector arrived, he was more nervous than I was.

"I've never inspected a distillery before," he admitted. He couldn't make sense of the manual either, and he didn't really know what he was supposed to be looking for. "You're the first person in western Carolina to apply for a distilling license in the last eighty years," he explained.

Millions of gallons of white lightning had come out of these mountains in those eighty years. Thousands of gallons were still coming out every year. I was the first person foolish enough to make it legal.

The only problem the inspector found was my records. In order to get a distilling license, *you had to already be distilling*. Since distilling without a license was illegal, the applicant was required to keep track of every drop of illegal liquor they distilled. I had done that. I had recorded every batch of moonshine I had run since I convinced John to let me set up shop at Pleasant Valley Farm more than one year ago.

"It indicates here that you've made a lot more whiskey than I see on the property," the inspector said.

John had built shelves all the way up the inside of his red-brick grain silo. We had close to three hundred quarts of whiskey stored in there, labeled by batch number. Looking up from the bottom, it was a glorious tower of jars, like a medieval cathedral of moonshine.

But I remembered all those afternoons sipping moonshine with Benny, John, and his brothers. The half-dozen thank-you pet 'n' pokes I'd given Forrest Jarrett, even though he'd never come by the farm. I had spent the spring and early summer going to the Western North Carolina Farmers Market and buying whatever fruit was in season: strawberries, peaches, nectarines. I'd talked Luke into helping me cut it up—is there any person less interested in helping around the house than a seventeen-year-old boy?—and we'd stuffed the fruit wedges into moonshine jars to experiment with "brandy for the ladies," as Forrest had called it way back when. I knew the inspector was right. Although I'd never sold a thimbleful of moonshine, we were dozens of jars short.

"We ran out of storage room," I said, "so we poured a bunch out. I should have marked that down."

The inspector stared at me. I knew that he knew that statement was at best partially true, and he knew I knew that, too. "Okay." He shrugged. "You pass."

I was so excited, I called my friend Lang Guenther, the man I'd been bugging with permit questions for the past year. "I'm coming to see you," I said.

"What?"

"I passed my inspection. I'm bringing my application to you in Cincinnati."

There was silence. A *long* silence. Then: "I've been doing this job for twenty-eight years. Nobody has ever come to see me."

"Well, get ready, because I'm coming, as soon as I can."

The federal license was tied to a specific address. I wasn't too keen on that address being "third shed on the left-hand side of the hill, Peaceful Valley Farm," but that was a small consideration. It was relatively easy to extend my license to a new facility, if and when I had one ready. The new place just had to pass inspection.

More important was my brand. I listed my corporate entity on the application as "Asheville Distilling Company," a nice generic back-office name. That blandness would never do for my products, though. My goal was to create not only the world's best heirloom moonshine, but a line of whiskeys. The name I put on all those bottles mattered.

I had been thinking of my brand for months, trying to figure

out the best approach. Serious? Old-fashioned? Funny? Weird?
I tested names on Luke while we sliced peaches and plums, but
he just rolled his eyes. *Whatever, Mom. I need to go work out.*

Marshall, though, took an interest. He suggested Marshall
and Listening Thinkers Distillery. I checked the acronym.
MALT Distillery.

Catchy. Meaningful. But not quite right.

"What about the name Tribute?" I asked him when I'd nar-
rowed down the choices.

"Love teaches us to listen to those that went thoughtfully
before," he wrote. "Marshall loves Tribute."

In the end, I chose a brand that meant something to me:
Troy & Sons. That name is the essence of my passion and my
life. My boys are the reason for everything I do.

Below the name, I added: "Established 1986."

Nineteen eighty-six was the year Marshall was born. It was
the year that buckled my life but also made me who I am.
"Before 1986" was cut off from me forever; "after 1986" was
a long series of steps that led me to Asheville, moonshine, and a
pure heart. It was Marshall and Coulton who had given shape
to that life. It was Luke who had inspired me to reach for more,
even when I was already overwhelmed.

"I'm coming," I told Lang when the final decision was made.
"I'll be there tomorrow."

The next morning, Charlie drove me to Cincinnati, an eight-
hour trip. He dropped me off at a nondescript office building
and told me he'd wait in the car. "You'll do better on your
own," he said.

I kissed him. I went inside. Lang Guenther was waiting for
me in a small windowless conference room that looked like an
employee break area, sans soda machine. He looked stunned
that I'd actually driven all that way.

"I just had a few questions on my application," I said, pulling out two copies of the fifty-page document.

Lang looked it over. "Well, I see a problem here," he said. "And here. And here . . ."

For the next two hours, Lang Guenther and I went over my application for a federal distilling permit. I had all my approvals and addendums, but the form was full of esoteric codes. "That's supposed to be a 386.9c, not a 398j," Lang would say, or something to that effect. "But don't worry, I'll fix it for you."

By the end, I had a perfect application, in duplicate, as required by law. "It says the process takes ninety days," I said.

Lang thought for a second. "I can get it back to you in six weeks," he said. It pays, *always,* to have a personal touch.

We walked together to the elevator, and I stepped on, as excited as I've ever been. As the doors were closing, I saw Lang standing in the hallway, looking sad to see me go. After all, he'd been answering my questions for more than a year, and in a way, we'd become friends. I stopped the doors, jumped out, and gave him a hug. "Thank you, Lang," I said.

"Sorry if I smell like men's cologne," I told Charlie when I got back to the car. He smiled. I kissed him again. "I got it," I said. "Troy & Sons is going to be legit."

It was September 27, 2010, our twenty-fifth wedding anniversary. We drove two blocks to Graeter's for a celebratory ice-cream cone. Then we drove home to the boys. The drive took ten hours, because it was pouring rain the whole way.

Six weeks later, I received my federal permit. I was the first woman licensed in the state of North Carolina to distill hard liquor, and only the fourth woman licensed in the entire United States.

I had done it. Through hard work and perseverance, and by

finding the right help, I had done it. I should have been happy. I was happy. I was ecstatic.

Which is why it hit me so hard when Charlie asked me, nervously, a few weeks later, "So, Troy . . . umm, do you have any money in your personal savings account? Because . . . umm . . . I need it."

Oh no, I thought. *Whisper Mountain.*

CHAPTER 22

BROKEN

I wasn't naive. I knew Whisper Mountain was over budget and underselling, and I knew the financial crisis had hit the real estate market hard. I had figured there were rough times ahead. We had put our house in Asheville up for sale in 2006, before the market started to soften. We didn't need a big house; we needed security for the boys. But we ended up chasing the market down. Every time we lowered the price, the market dropped lower.

Still, I was caught by surprise when Charlie said we were broke. He'd put everything we had into Whisper Mountain.

"What do you mean, *everything*?"

Our savings. His income. The profit from selling Angelwood. Everything we'd worked for our whole life. Everything.

I understood why he did it. Charlie had taken out a massive loan to buy and develop the property. He had leveraged up, borrowing far more than we possessed. It was the method he'd used to great success in Texas. But this time, he'd gotten trapped. Property at Whisper Mountain hadn't been selling for years, and the interest rate on the loan was going to balloon. So he'd taken all our money and paid off the debt. It left us free and clear on Whisper Mountain, but we no longer had money for our mortgage. Or Luke's college. Or Marshall and Coulton's health care.

"Oh God, can we sell Whisper Mountain?"

Charlie shook his head. Almost every development in Western North Carolina had gone bankrupt. They were selling out of foreclosure for nothing, and the new owners were dumping properties at cut-rate prices. If we tried to sell Whisper Mountain, we'd get pennies back for every dollar we'd invested. There wouldn't be enough money to keep us afloat. Not for long, anyway, and not if we wanted to keep the boys with us for the rest of their lives.

And if we sold Whisper Mountain, what would we have to make money on in the future? Nothing.

Nothing but my moonshine.

I could feel the weight as the realization set in. I could feel my desperation and despair. I had always followed my father's lead. My whole life, Dad had been my inspiration. I had wanted to be an entrepreneur because he was an entrepreneur. I had wanted to do things his way: by the seat of my pants, with passion, and never taking no for an answer.

But in the end, Dad had failed. That's what I had forgotten. Dad had founded the first Spanish-language radio station in Houston. It was a huge success . . . until a mysterious fire burned down the radio tower. Soon after, a hurricane devastated South Texas, forcing his insurance company to collapse. In less than six months, Dad lost it all: the ranch, the cattle, the Lincoln. At the end of his life, he was living in a small apartment in Houston, almost penniless.

There's always been a small part of me that thinks he gave up. I think that might have been why he said to Charlie a few days before his heart attack: "I'd still be happy if I died now, because I've lived seven lives."

He was working on ideas for two new businesses. I found plans in the apartment, when I helped Mom clean out Dad's things. But I'm not sure his heart was in it. He was sixty. He was broke. He wanted, in theory, to take another shot. But I'm not sure he had the energy to go through the battles again.

I've never been angry at Dad for this. He was a good man and a great father. He didn't owe me anything. He'd already given me more, through his example and love, than he could ever have given me in dollars and cents. All his children were grown. He had only himself and Mom, and Mom could take care of herself. Dad could go whenever he wanted, doing whatever he believed in.

My life wasn't like that. Luke would one day be independent. He was seventeen; he was almost independent already. But Marshall and Coulton were dependent on me today, tomorrow, and every day for the rest of their lives. Nobody would ever love them like Charlie and me. Nobody would ever care for them in the same way. They were pure souls; they deserved good lives.

I had let them down.

John McEntire was my partner in making whiskey. I'd told him so that summer. Before I left Peaceful Valley Farm, I would promise him a share of any revenue I earned from the moonshine we had developed together.

But Troy & Sons was bigger than product development, and it was bigger than moonshine. It was my lifelong dream. It was the pure heart of what I'd always wanted to do. I wanted to have a business. Make something of my own. Make it great.

Make it mine. All the things I had learned in the last twenty-four years as a mother, they were in my moonshine: patience, determination, strength, care with details, joy in the little things, and love.

Most of all, love.

I thought that was Troy & Sons' purpose: to distill and preserve the values I had learned to cherish. Now, suddenly, I realized Troy & Sons had to do much more than that.

It had to save my family.

PART IV

Taccirring

THERE IS A QUIET LOVELY GOLDEN DREAM ABOVE.

ARE YOU THERE?

ARE YOU DREAMING OF YOUR PERFECT LOVE?

CHAPTER 23

TAKING STOCK

It is unfair to blame Charlie for the disaster at Whisper Mountain. I am a partner in my marriage—an *equal* partner, as every woman should be—so I take responsibility. I had gone along with Charlie's plan to buy a mountain, and I had approved the plan without studying the financial arrangements. I knew he was funneling the money from sales of lots at Whisper Mountain back into the project, but I didn't know he had started funneling our savings into it, too.

I should have known. It was my responsibility to know. But I hadn't paid as much attention as I should have. Over the years, as I devoted myself to caring for our boys, I had made a common mistake: I let the finances become primarily my husband's responsibility. I didn't realize our personal savings were tied up in Whisper Mountain. I didn't know we were risking our financial security. But I should have. I knew Charlie was doing what Dad had advised at the start of our marriage, but I didn't know the stakes had gotten too high.

I don't expect anyone to feel sorry for me. I had been living the American dream. Charlie had worked his way up the corporate ladder; he had been paid handsomely to supervise the building of high-rises, shopping centers, and enormous commercial campuses. He had used that experience to start a successful development business. He had taken care of us. That's why I was able to devote myself to the boys. That's why I was able to save enough money to pursue my own dream. The comforts and opportunities we had all those years, they were the result of Charlie's ingenuity and hard work.

Then he . . . well, he got caught in a force nobody understood at the time, a force that warped the normal shape of society and pulled millions of Americans down. Where there was unscrupulous behavior by Wall Street and banks, and there was certainly unscrupulous behavior, we were victims. Where there was overconfidence, we were complicit. Where there was foolish risk-taking, we were guilty. The banks were handing out money, and we took it. Shysters on Wall Street conspired to give us the rope, but we hanged ourselves. I had no one to blame but myself.

It's just that . . . well, Charlie and I had disagreed on Whisper Mountain for years. Even now I find my resentment bubbling up, not for the bad investment—that was a product of the times—but because my husband didn't listen. I never thought I'd be the kind of woman whose voice was ignored, but Charlie . . . he didn't listen to me. I warned him he was spending too much on infrastructure. I told him it was taking too long to get the amenities in place. I advised him to work in smaller pieces, selling a section of the project before spending money to develop the rest.

No, he was the expert. This was his development. He was

going to do things his way, and that meant everything was going to be top-notch. Other developers were cutting corners to make a quick buck. Charlie was never going to do that. Charlie was going to build things right.

Fine. I understood. He had spent his whole life learning his trade. And he was good. He knew how to build a solid road up a steep mountain far better than I did.

It was the sales end that crushed me, because I had always been our expert on sales. I was the one who sold our properties in the 1980s. I was the one who marketed our environmentally friendly developments outside Austin, Texas. After Charlie built Michael Dell's house, I used our connection with the family (lovely people, always welcoming to Marshall and Coulton) to become Michael Dell's go-to real estate agent, helping executives find properties when they relocated to Austin. It was only a few families a year, a few weeks of work, but these were big deals, and I did them right. I was never a full-time real estate agent, but I was *good* at that job. No; I was great at it.

Charlie didn't listen to me on sales at Whisper Mountain. He had his own ideas about timing and development. He had his own plans for marketing. Instead of relying on me, he hired a husband-and-wife team to do sales. I never liked or trusted them, but even when sales were slow, Charlie stuck with them.

I knew things weren't right. There was no way Whisper Mountain should have been languishing in 2007 when mountain real estate was booming. Charlie realized, eventually, there was a problem.

"The wife is pregnant," he sighed. "I can't pressure them now. Once they have the baby, I'll talk to them."

Aaargh. Just like a softhearted man—and bless him, Charlie has always been kind. Listen to the woman who cries and makes excuses, not the one telling you to toughen up.

It turned out the couple was not doing right by us. We were paying them a salary to work full-time and exclusively for us, but they had an ownership stake in a competing development a few miles away and were using Whisper Mountain to identify leads. More than forty lots were sold at the other development. Twenty more sales at Whisper Mountain would have paid off our loans and set us free.

Charlie fired them. They had done wrong by other people, too, and they are now under federal indictment for a different case. But by the time Charlie acted, it was too late. I had left for my shed at Peaceful Valley Farm, and the real estate market had cratered.

Did I know about the problems when I started distilling in 2009? Yes. And no. You would have had to be living in a cave in 2009 not to know that real estate had gone belly-up and the economy had plunged into a severe recession. It was on the news every night, and it was in front of my eyes. For Sale signs stayed up in good neighborhoods, like the For Sale sign in my own front yard. Houses went into foreclosure. Businesses closed, including Tomato Jam. I never knew the restaurant was in trouble. One morning, the doors were locked. By the time I realized it was closed for good, Charlie and Rebecca had packed their bags, as well as their young daughter, and moved to California. I haven't heard from them since.

But things weren't *that* bad in Buncombe County. Downtown Asheville stayed strong. Before the recession, the area was so hot, there was a shortage of housing and retail space. There were plans for a massive building boom, but unlike with the Depression, this time the fates were kind; the recession hit before everyone broke ground. The new projects died in the planning stages, and good ol' Asheville stayed true to what it was: a small, laid-back mountain town. The stores and bars and restaurants in downtown weren't outposts of national chains, they were parts of our lives. They were owned by neighbors and friends, and we supported them. The mood wasn't festive in 2009—even the street musicians formed a collaborative to help each other through tough times (so Asheville!)—but most of the businesses dug in and held on.

So I wasn't too concerned in May 2009, when I started working with John McEntire. Charlie and I had been investing in property for thirty years. We had been through real estate busts before. They were always short-lived. In the past, we had simply stayed the course and come out ahead.

By the time Charlie came to me in 2010, though, it was clear the market wasn't coming back. I believe Forrest Jarrett is right: good people will come back to the mountains. But in rural Madison and Buncombe Counties, they were leaving like it was the Great Depression all over again. There was no way in that environment, *no way*, that we would sell enough property at a high enough price to avoid financial ruin.

Charlie was crushed. I was crushed, too, obviously. I was deeply distraught. I cursed Charlie to the ground, often when I was alone in the car, where the boys couldn't hear. A few times, I drove Charlie around town, just so I could vent at him. Sometimes Charlie argued back. Often, he just took my anger. He was heartbroken. That was clear. I had never seen my husband so down. I had never seen him without a smile on his face. But after he finally admitted where we were, Charlie fell into a depression so deep he could barely function.

But damn it, Charlie needed to get going. We needed to put our backs into this problem, both of us, because so much was on the line.

Luke was two years from college. We had adopted him. We had taken him into our hearts and our lives. We owed him an education. But if worst came to worst, he could get loans. He could get a job. He could survive on his own. Marshall and Coulton needed thousands of dollars of care each month, every month, for the rest of their lives. Charlie and I should have worked with a professional to set that money aside in a safe investment. One that would grow slowly, without risk of catastrophic loss. But we hadn't done it. We hadn't set any money aside. It had all gone to Whisper Mountain.

Of all my stupid, irresponsible decisions . . .

I tried not to think of the worst-case scenario as I bathed Coulton or sat with Marshall at his alphabet board. I tried not to think of Charlie and me dead, hopefully of old age. Mom gone. Luke successful, with a young family but no free money or time. The boys forced into a state home. Coulton strapped to a bed because he thrashed so much. Marshall ignored because he was so calm, and moved so little, that the $10-an-hour health care workers would assume his mind wasn't there.

I tried not to think of the story Charlie had read of an older couple with a special needs son. The wife had advanced Alzheimer's; the husband couldn't care for both of them on his own. He shot his boy, then his wife, then himself.

It was a nightmare. It was a cry of despair that didn't seem possible but didn't quite seem impossible, either. Every parent of a special needs child dreads it: the day they can no longer personally provide the necessary care. There are some situations for our children, we know in our hearts, worse than death.

People have asked me, over the years, if I was angry with Charlie. Didn't I want to kill him?

No, I never wanted to kill Charlie. I wanted to divorce him, I say now with a laugh. I never came close to following through. I love Charlie too much. He is a good man and, despite his one mistake, a good husband. I had married a bad man once. I'd had a man I thought I loved knock me down the stairs and almost break my neck. So I never took Charlie for granted.

And the boys needed him. Where would they be—where would any of us be—without Charlie's love?

I knew he was hurting. I knew he never intended to put our family at risk. He should have stopped paying the bank loans. That, in hindsight, was the crushing mistake. He should have let Whisper Mountain go into foreclosure, instead of plunging our savings down the hole. Everyone else had done just that and walked away. But that wasn't Charlie. He believed in honesty and effort. He wasn't going to cut corners or break promises, even to banks. The qualities that made him successful, and made me love him, were the ones that ultimately made him fail.

But that failure was between us now. It lived with us. There were many days when I couldn't look at Charlie and he couldn't look at me. There were days I didn't want to be in the same room with him, or even in the same house. For three years, starting at the moment he told me where the money had gone, I couldn't go to Whisper Mountain. I didn't even want to think about it. Not because I was angry. Or not *only* because I was angry.

Because I was sad. I was heartbroken over what had happened to us.

But I put that heartbreak away. I kept it behind closed doors, where only I could feel the pain. Maybe that wasn't healthy, but it was necessary. I couldn't just rely on Charlie. Not anymore. If I was going to save my family—and I *was* going to save my family—I had to lift that crushing weight and become the strong, successful businesswoman I had always wanted to be.

No excuses. No weakness. Why is a whine, as I had always

told myself. I had always believed in what I was doing at Peaceful Valley Farm. I knew in my soul Troy & Sons was going to be a successful brand. What changed, when Charlie told me we were so far underwater even a submarine couldn't save us, was the timeline. It takes a lot of hard work to build a company from scratch. I had figured I had a decade, maybe more.

Now, I realized, I had less than a year.

Fortunately, I had Oscar.

CHAPTER 24

OSCAR

I had heard of Oscar Wong long before I met him. We had acquaintances in common, and he was a local legend, the kind of person friends point out with admiration. If you think of Asheville as an alternative town, a cool place to drink great beer on a patio, listen to up-and-coming bands, and hang out with artistic people who don't want to be shoved down a traditional career path, you're thinking of the town Oscar Wong helped create.

Oscar wasn't an Asheville hipster. He was a structural engineer who had owned a company in Charlotte that built nuclear waste facilities. A few years after he sold his company, he was approached by John Lyda, a home beer brewer looking for capital to turn his hobby into a business. Oscar liked the young man, and he loved the beer. He said, "If you want to start a business in Charlotte, then no. I'll pass. But if you want to try Asheville, I'm interested." Oscar and his wife had recently bought a retirement cabin in the mountains, and they were looking to settle down there.

Highland Brewing Company started production in the basement of a pizza restaurant in 1994. It was the first legal brewery in Western North Carolina since Prohibition, and Oscar was its owner and champion. For the first four years, the company only produced kegs and hand-filled bottles. For the first eight years, it didn't make a profit. In 2002, Oscar bought a used bottling line and began to produce in bulk. By then, the company's commitment to quality beer and giving back to the community had become synonymous with the "new" Asheville.

By 2010, Asheville was being hailed as one of America's great beer towns, with fifteen independent breweries and numerous brewpubs serving local lagers and IPAs. Highland Brewing was still the largest and most beloved. The company was a point of pride for the community—a symbol of what Asheville had become and what every local entrepreneur aspired to be. Oscar Wong, then seventy, was commonly referred to as the "godfather" of the Asheville brewing scene. In reality, he was godfather to a generational wave of locally owned, philanthropically inclined, gourmet craft businesses.

Oscar and I met at a charity event in spring 2010, about six months before Charlie broke the devastating news about Whisper Mountain. We hit it off right away, since we were both entrepreneurs at a traditional retirement age, and neither of us was exactly Asheville hip. I'm forever a Vandy girl, and Oscar still dresses like an engineer in tan slacks and plain button-down shirts. More importantly, we each have a special needs adult child. It's not lost on me that two of my most important supporters, John McEntire and Oscar Wong, had this in common with me, and I don't think it was a coincidence.

We share decades of similar frustrations and joys, and we share an understanding of daily, lifelong commitment. We love, without expecting acknowledgment. We give, because being able to give is a gift. We trust each other, because we know how loyalty to our children has changed us. John McEntire understood my need to be with Coulton in the hospital, because he would have done the same for Lindsey. That's why he wasn't bothered that I forgot to call him for two months after my first corn order. I think Oscar Wong understood my work ethic and values in the same way.

I mentioned, at some point, that I had spent the last two years learning to distill whiskey, mostly in the mountains with old moonshiners and in a shack in the country with a corn farmer. Oscar was intrigued. He said I should bring some of my whiskey by his office. Maybe it was only small talk at a social function; I don't know. Oscar may have thought, as Pat Whalen had, that I wouldn't follow up.

I followed up. I called Oscar every few days for a month. I sent him e-mails and texts. He was a busy man, but he made time for me. So that summer, while I was nailing down my final inspections, I drove over to the Highland Brewing complex with a quart jar of my moonshine. I gave it to Oscar. He drank a spiderleg. He was pleasantly surprised.

In fact, he loved it.

I was still working with Pat Whalen on my business plan. I spoke the language of business, but I didn't have spreadsheets of my costs, pricing, discounts, or profit margins projected for one year, two years, and five years down the road. I had settled on a brand name and created a great whiskey, but I had no idea how many employees I would need or what my sales force would look like. Fortunately, Oscar's entrepreneurial style was more Dad than Pat. He had founded Highland Brewing because he believed in the quality of John Lyda's beer, then used the next eight years to sort out the rest.

In the end, Oscar Wong didn't help me because he liked my numbers. He did it because he loved my moonshine.

The thing about creating something from scratch—anything—is that you never know how good it is until you share it. You believe in it, because you've worked so hard. Then, at the moment it leaves your hand, you suddenly doubt. You're terrified. John and I thought we had produced a great product, but we'd been hanging out in a small shed in rural North Carolina for fourteen months, sipping batch after batch of hard liquor. For all we knew, we'd gone crazy out there. We might have been distilling corn vinegar.

When Oscar Wong tasted my moonshine and loved it, that's the moment I knew I'd created something special. A great liquor, yes, but something of my own, too.

Oscar put together a small investment group to offer significant backing, and I brought in four of my best female friends—Aan and Carol from Texas, Rosie, and Meredith, a sorority sister from college—to supplement their funds. Thanks to this seed capital and Oscar's financial backing, Asheville Distilling was able to secure a bank loan at a good rate. So by the time I received my distilling permit and Charlie broke his news, I already had the financing needed to create a real distillery.

The best thing Oscar's financial backing did, honestly, was take away any thought of turning back. I remember Oscar joking, "You could probably buy me out of my business, if you wanted." I just laughed. Awkwardly. He thought I was rich because I owned a mountain.

In reality, I was scraping bottom. The money for the distillery couldn't be used for personal expenses, and I wasn't getting paid a salary, meaning I'd make no money until my moonshine hit the market. That meant six, seven, ten months of tooth grinding and penny pinching. If Oscar had known how broke I was at that moment, he might have flinched. But I never gave him a reason to doubt. I was confident that with hard work, faith, a pure heart, and a little luck, we had a clear path to success. If I could keep on it. And keep going. And the money didn't run out.

I had been looking for a permanent home for the distillery since the spring. I wanted a large raw space, preferably in a historic building downtown. My goal was to make my distillery part of the fabric of Asheville, and that meant being in the center. Pat Whalen helped me with that search, but rents were high, despite the recession. North Carolina doesn't allow distilleries to sell from their tasting rooms, denying me the primary income stream a downtown location would provide. Once I found out about our personal financial situation, that dream was dead.

But Oscar came through once again. Highland Brewing had recently purchased a warehouse complex on the east side of Asheville and expanded its bottling operation. The rest of the complex contained a ball bearing manufacturer, a velour wholesaler, and several empty spaces with loading docks. Oscar offered me a space.

I took Charlie with me to inspect it. He was a construction and permitting expert, after all, and I knew I couldn't build and run the entire business alone. It may seem that, as I crossed hurdles—getting a permit, perfecting a whiskey—my Post-it walls of tasks would have gotten cleaner. In fact, the opposite was happening. My home office was exploding with Post-it notes. They were everywhere—floor, ceiling, on the back of the door. It seemed the more work I did, the more work I needed to do.

Bringing in Charlie was natural. For one thing, I didn't have to pay him. For another, he was my soul mate. I was mad at him, of course, but I couldn't let that stand in the way. I needed Charlie's brainpower and ingenuity to help me pull the family together. If he wasn't going to be working at dead-quiet Whisper Mountain, he could at least be consulting for me.

Asheville is a gorgeous town. You almost can't help having a view of the mountains. But Oscar had managed to find an ugly spot. The area was heavily industrial, bordered by a paint and body shop, a biogas facility, and a yard where the county parked its maintenance equipment. Oscar's warehouse complex was up a short wooded drive, but the forest was filled with poison ivy. The building was low and flat, without a view past the trees. The most visible features were the large parking lot, the twelve loading docks, and a massive tower that held up the power lines from the local transformer.

The space available was in the middle of the almost-two-acre-long building, but it had an exterior corner where the line of the building jogged back. That gave it a large front wall and a smaller side wall with exterior access, but it was set up for industrial work, so it had no windows. The entrance was a metal safety door. Only one light worked inside, but it was enough to see that one of the interior walls was collapsing, probably from a leak in the roof. The space was filthy, and the air smelled of mold.

"It's got some hair on it," Charlie commented, making Oscar laugh.

It wasn't what I wanted. Not at all. But it had potential. Highland Brewing was planning to open a tasting room in the space next door, which might bring foot traffic. There was a loading garage, and the highway was only a mile away. There was plenty of room for an office, distilling equipment, a couple hundred whiskey barrels, and a warehouse full of moonshine. I didn't want a fancy operation, but I needed my distillery to look like a real company, not a mom-and-pop operation. This space could do that.

And I could afford it.

"You think you could make it work, Charlie?"

Charlie nodded. This was a project he could handle.

We set to work immediately cleaning and clearing. It was a family affair, with Luke coming after school to help Charlie haul and dispose of debris. We settled on a minimalist plan to divide the space into two sections: a small tasting room on the corner with a wall of windows that faced Highland Brewing, and a large bare-bones distillery-warehouse area. The workspace was twenty-six feet high, so I needed high ventilation windows in the exterior wall that could be opened with cranks to release the distilling vapors. The back area would be for bottling, labeling, and storing my stock. The center, under the ventilation windows and visible from the tasting room, would be filled with my industrial-size moonshine still, mash cookers, and fermentation chambers.

Of course, I didn't have any of that equipment. At the moment, all I had were a few food-grade barrels of mash and Colonel Wilson's sixty-gallon still pumping out moonshine in my eighteen-by-twenty-foot shed at Peaceful Valley Farm.

I decided to order a larger two-hundred-gallon still from Colonel Wilson. It was a stopgap; it would never produce as much whiskey as I wanted. But if I got it cranking full-time, it would create enough revenue to eventually pay for a real pot still.

When I mentioned my plan to Oscar, he shook his head. For the most part, he wasn't active in the day-to-day decisions of the company. His preferred role at Asheville Distilling was to be available to answer questions. Believe me, I had a lot of them. Asking for advice, eagerly and often, was one of my best attributes.

"Don't buy cheap equipment because you're just starting out," Oscar told me. "Buy the best and the biggest and believe in yourself. It's cheaper in the long run. I learned that lesson the hard way."

He was right. I'd wasted money on my current Colonel Wilson still. It had only arrived a few months before, and I already needed something larger. Now I was about to make that exact same mistake again. Fortunately, Oscar had reminded me of the importance of forward-thinking business decisions. Don't solve today's problem by creating a bigger problem tomorrow.

"I don't know anything about industrial distilling equipment," I said.

"The Germans make the best equipment," Oscar replied.

Fine. Done. I started researching German manufacturers of industrial distilling equipment. Then I set to work making sure I had everything in place to use the equipment, whenever it arrived.

CHAPTER 25

TRUST

The hard-spirit industry is excessively regulated, and my eight-month odyssey to get my distilling license was only a foot in the door. The government still needed to "certify my formulation," meaning they would analyze the ingredients to make sure my moonshine qualified as whiskey. Moonshine is an attitude, not a liquor category; it is not listed on government or industry forms. The term "whiskey" is used for an alcohol derived from a grain mash. That was the category I needed to apply for.

The government also had to approve my labels and informational material, so I'd been working with a marketing consultant (a woman, of course) to create my basic label since the spring. I wanted a classic design that evoked the early twentieth century, when moonshining was a craft. This meant muted colors, a type-heavy design, and space to hand-write the batch number on each bottle. We ended up with a plain tan label featuring traditional (and slightly feminine) leaflike etchings and, in the top center, a small crest. The crest was an S over a T, with a horse on each side.

The largest text was the brand: Troy & Sons. The hardest decision was the next line. I wanted to call the product moonshine, because that's what it was. Pat Whalen, Oscar, my marketing consultant: everyone was concerned. Moonshine was considered cheap and low quality. It was the liquor in the jug marked "XXX" that might make you go blind.

I was making a high-end spirit for the top shelf, not a cheap option hidden under the bar. So maybe I should call it white whiskey, the traditional term for unaged whiskey? Would that make buyers think quality?

I didn't like it. I'd spent all this time making moonshine, not white whiskey, so why hold back now?

I decided to go with "Platinum Whiskey," a term that sounded highbrow without actually meaning anything. Underneath it, I wrote "Heirloom Moonshine," because that is exactly what it was. I doubted buyers would know the phrase meant moonshine made in the style popular before mob-backed 'shiners started adding sugar and pumping it out en masse, but at least the word "heirloom" would imply craft and tradition.

I sent the labels, forms, and "liquor specimens" to the government the day I received my license. Then I headed to the American Distilling Institute trade show.

I had a lot to do at the show: make contacts; meet distributors; figure out how, where, and when to market my product. Most importantly, I needed bottles to put my moonshine in. I met with a dozen manufacturers, saw countless options, and decided on a design that was narrow front to back and broader at the top than the base. It reminded me of old medicine bottles, a popular container for early moonshiners. With its broad shoulders and narrow base, it also looked feminine, as if modeled after a woman's torso. Those are the qualities I always gravitate toward: something nostalgic and crafted, with the strength and grace of a woman.

After the bottle was chosen, I met with cork merchants, since I wanted everything top-shelf, no caps. Then I met with companies that printed labels and companies that made machines for applying labels to bottles. I needed racks and barrels, because John McEntire and I were developing a recipe for traditional aged whiskey using heirloom Crooked Creek corn and Turkey Red wheat. I'd have to store it three years in oak barrels, but I figured I'd have plenty of time for a few runs on my new German industrial still, especially in the early months when sales would be slow.

By November, it was time to decide on a still, and once again I leaned on Charlie. While I was working on labels and supplies, I had sent Charlie on a tour of distilleries. What Charlie lacked in experience, he made up for in technical expertise, not to mention likability. He talked his way into the back rooms of major whiskey and bourbon producers in Tennessee and Kentucky, where he could see their real equipment, not the pot stills they had on show for their tours. Our fellow distillers were generous with their time. They answered Charlie's technical questions, and a few even allowed him to work with the equipment, watched closely by a master distiller, of course.

We were leaning toward Kothe, a respected company that could provide everything I needed, from the pot still to the distilling towers and storage tanks. I didn't want to buy without seeing them, though, and I didn't have time to visit the factory in Germany. So the final step in the evaluation process was a three-day workshop in Chicago where I could learn about distilling on a professional Kothe system. I took Charlie, of course, because he already knew more than me about industrial distilling. If building and maintaining these multipart systems were technical puzzles, then Charlie was my expert.

That class was like graduation, the final chance to put the finishing touches on my craft. The instructor taught us about enzymes that would make large runs consistent, a vital consideration for commercial liquor distillers. He taught us how to balance temperature, time, and pressure on a Kothe machine. He even advised me on grains that could be combined with Crooked Creek corn, because if the moonshine had any success I'd run through the world's supply of Crooked Creek pretty quickly. John and I had been working to find the right grain to supplement his corn, and I had contracted with a few other farmers to grow Crooked Creek the next summer. We had the right recipe. We had the right ingredients. We had already proven we could distill. The Chicago workshop showed me how to do things at a commercial scale.

At the end of the weekend, I was sold. I ordered a two-thousand-liter Kothe distillation system, made to order in Germany and scheduled for delivery in the spring.

I was also sold on Charlie. I can't say we worked everything out during that weekend, but it was the first time in recent memory that we felt completely comfortable together. We laughed and enjoyed ourselves as we made whiskey, and at the end of each day, we went out for a quiet dinner near the hotel. It wasn't fancy, but it was just the two of us, alone and making small talk, for the first time in years.

Looking back, I can see that Whisper Mountain had been between us for a long time, probably as far back as the sale of Angelwood. Our world had fragmented at that moment. We had gone our separate ways and pursued our own dreams, but now we were coming back together. The idea of turning over my whiskey distilling to someone else, after everything I'd done, might seem ludicrous. But it was necessary. I couldn't run a business, sell my products, and manufacture them as well. Not on the scale I wanted. I had to trust someone.

It could have been John McEntire, I suppose, but that wasn't his style. He didn't want to leave his farm and throw himself full-time into Troy & Sons. He already had a life he loved.

It had to be Charlie. I had to give him that trust and responsibility, even though he'd broken my heart. And when I did, to my surprise, I could feel that heart starting to mend.

CHAPTER 26

WINTER

I threw an eightieth-birthday party for Forrest Jarrett just before Thanksgiving 2010. His guy friends were absolutely no help in planning, so I told Forrest to give me his invitation list. It was fifty people long, and that was "cutting to the nub," as Forrest put it. I knew everybody would show up. When Forrest threw a party, everybody came.

The party was supposed to be a dinner in my house's formal dining room, but it devolved quickly into drinking and story-telling. I don't think Forrest knows how to sit down, but he sure knew how to get down. He had some good dance moves for an octogenarian in ostrich-skin boots. I was legal and paying taxes, even though I wasn't bottling, so the moonshine was flowing. I went to bed to the sound of bluegrass music on the stereo and Forrest Jarrett holding court on my back porch.

The next evening, I met the men from Forrest's breakfast group at the bottom of Jarrett Farm Road. I'd found a bunch of large stones in the woods and had one of Forrest's friends haul them to the only stonecutter in the area, who carved head-stones. He carved one of Forrest's famous sayings into each stone:

HAVE A SPIDERLEG.

MAMBLY PAMBLY

HUBBLE UP!

I CAN'T BELIEVE I'VE LIVED THIS CLEAN A LIFE.

I'M GOING TO STAY WITH YA UNTIL I SEE YA GOING DOWN.

BEST I'VE SEEN, AND I'VE SEEN A THOUSAND.

"First time I've carved for someone alive," the stonecutter remarked when we went to pick them up.

We drove down to Forrest's pond in a caravan with the stones in the back of a pickup truck, honking our horns and scaring the bejesus out of Forrest's poor wife. It took an hour to arrange the stones into a seating area around the fire pit. Forrest just shook his head, flabbergasted at what we'd done. He had a tear in his eye, and he wasn't ashamed to cry. We lit a fire against the bitter cold and drank a few spiderlegs. I felt like I'd done something right, like I knew Forrest well enough to give him what he really wanted: a monument to himself, sure, but one his friends could park their asses on and tell him he was full of it. I felt, that night, like I belonged.

We received an offer on our house soon after. That was our crack of light. If we could get out from under our payments and into something cheaper . . .

Unfortunately, the offer was less than our outstanding loan, and we didn't have the money to pay the difference. I thought the bank would help us. We had paid off millions of dollars in loans on Whisper Mountain—literally millions—when everyone else was walking away. I thought that would count for something.

I was naive. The bank didn't care. They wouldn't even answer our phone calls. They had a system, we were told. They'd let us know.

Soon after, the CAP program said it was cutting support for the boys. It seemed to happen every year, when the weather turned cold. The CAP program said they needed to cut back, then made us go through an onerous fight to prove Marshall and Coulton still needed special care. As the recession progressed, though, the proposed cuts became more severe. This was doubly traumatic since many recipients, including us, were struggling through their own financial crisis. We hadn't been dependent on funding from CAP in years past; this year, on the verge of personal bankruptcy, I was desperate for it.

I had just steeled for the fight when Oscar asked, "How's the label approval going?"

"I haven't heard back," I said, realizing it had been six weeks.

I called the Alcohol and Tobacco Tax and Trade Bureau. They checked their files. "We never received your application," they said.

"Oh yes, you did."

I gave them my name and business title. I searched for my application numbers. Finally, after talking with half a dozen operators, one finally said: "Oh, that form. That was only to register your entity name. Common mistake. You need to submit another set of forms and specimens for your label approval."

So I filled out the new forms, grumbling the whole time. It took me three days I couldn't afford to waste. I sent everything to the new department I had to deal with, but their automated system wouldn't accept the application. I tried again. Rejected, again and again.

I called the TTB. I must have spoken with twenty IT specialists this time. It took hours, but nothing worked. Then: "What type of computer are you using?"

"An Apple."

"Oh, we're not compatible with Apple."

I was stunned. It was the end of 2010, less than a year before Steve Jobs died of pancreatic cancer after conquering the world. I didn't even know anyone still using a PC. And yet this governmental department wasn't compatible with Apple?!

It took me another wasted day to find a PC and transfer everything to new documents.

Then, after thirty days of anguished waiting and desperate calls, we finally heard back from the bank. The message was two words, relayed by the real estate agent: no sale.

By then, Christmas was approaching, clearly our last at the Big House. I had always loved Christmas, because it offered a break. Charlie was home, the family was gathered, and I could relax. It was a time to take Marshall and Coulton to the Western North Carolina Farmers Market and push them in their wheelchairs through five acres of Christmas trees. A time to remember how much nicer Christmas was in Asheville, with morning frost on the trees and often a layer of snow, than it had been in Austin, with its balmy weather and occasional rain.

I couldn't enjoy it, though, not like I had in the past. The scythe was over my head, and I had to force myself to focus on our traditions: Marshall's annual letter to family and friends; the yearly photograph of all three boys in their Christmas sweaters. I had to force myself not to think of the year Dad died during the holiday season, the year I realized good things can end and the things you love can be lost.

I bundled Coulton for his annual Christmas charity drive, Coulton's Cake Run. We drove to local bakeries to pick up donated baked goods, then we delivered them to the battered women's home and the veterans' homeless shelter. Coulton loved it. He rocked and made his happy sound. I felt selfish as I realized how lucky I was. The boys didn't need fancy presents. They didn't need a fancy house. Even Luke would be happy with a few dumbbells and a tiny room of his own; he'd never been into material things. We had each other. We had my mother and sister, who came up to the house around noon every Christmas. We sat all afternoon, with the older boys happily in someone's arms, talking and listening to Dad's old Christmas albums. For dinner, Mom made tenderloin and curried fruit, Marshall's favorite. At the shelters, Coulton's cakes might have been the only celebratory thing those poor suffering people would have for the holidays. Even if I ended up with nothing else, I had my family.

It doesn't relieve the pain to know others are suffering, especially at Christmas. It doesn't make things okay. But it does give you perspective, and that was something I needed. I knew how much the worry was piling up and crushing me. I *hurt* for what those other parents were going through, and I bathed Coulton with extra love and tenderness that night, massaging his stick arms as he sat strapped in his bathing seat in the shower, rocking enthusiastically and glancing around furtively, unable to stay focused on any one thing, even me. I hugged him tight as I laid him between the guardrails of his bed, thankful I could give him comfort. The doctors had told me Coulton and Marshall wouldn't live ten years, but it had been twenty-five, and I still had them both.

I received the e-mail regarding my label approval a week later. I sighed with relief when I saw it in my inbox, because without this approval, I was stuck. I wasn't allowed to market, bottle, or label my moonshine.

"Thank you for your application," the e-mail read. "Please note that because of unexpected volume your process will take approximately 120 additional days to complete."

I almost had a stroke. Another four months! That would put me into mid-April, assuming there were no other problems. Manufacturing the labels would take another two months. That put me in mid-June. And that mid-June date was just to get the materials to start packaging my moonshine. I'd still have to sort, fill, apply, ship . . .

I called Lang Guenther in a panic. "Lang! I have a problem, a major problem. I've been trying to get my label approved for three months, and I just got a notice that it's going to be another hundred and twenty days, and . . ."

Lang was calm, as always. He never seemed to get ruffled. "You should contact the head of TTB," he said. "His name is John Manfredo."

"How do I get in touch with him? What's his phone number?"

Lang laughed. "I can't tell you that, Troy, but you know my e-mail, right?"

"Yes. Of course."

Lang was quiet, waiting for me to figure it out, but my brain was scattered. "You know how my e-mail is put together, right?" he said.

Oh! Then I understood. If I knew how to e-mail someone named Lang Guenther, I knew how to e-mail someone named John Manfredo.

I spent most of the night composing my e-mail. I didn't want to sound frantic, but I needed Mr. Manfredo to understand the seriousness of my situation. I was a small business owner. I was a mother. I was a human being. I had spent a significant amount of time and money getting licensed, and I couldn't endure a seven-month approval process for labels. No small distillery could. I needed to save my family, not lose my business. They needed to help me. Or at least, they needed to not stand in my way.

I sent the e-mail the next morning, before driving Luke to school. I'm sure I was quiet the whole drive. The pressure of that moment: it felt like I was being squeezed, and there was no way to stop it. It felt like I was seconds away from my skull caving in.

Two hours later, I received a call from an executive at TTB apologizing for the problems. That afternoon, I had a conference call with the formulation and label divisions and the head of IT. I told them what it was like to go through the process; they listened and asked questions. I think (and hope) the process was improved for everyone who came after me.

I know it was for me. Three days later, I had my approvals.

Soon after, the full assistance package for the boys came through. I had another year of health support. One more year of freedom and opportunity.

I celebrated by flying to Mexico . . . to inspect a sample run of bottles at a manufacturing plant in an industrial wasteland outside Mexico City. I wanted to make them in the United States, but domestic companies didn't produce in the small runs I could afford. I had to cut every expense, and I had to move fast. It was the dead of winter, still snowy in the mountains, but spring was coming. It was time to start selling some moonshine.

CHAPTER 27

A WOMAN DID THIS?

I had all my government approvals, finally, but I still needed one other thing: distributors. By law, distillers can't sell directly to stores and restaurants. They must use a distributor. They can only have one distributor in a state; that distributor can *only* distribute inside that state, not across state lines. Each state must have a different distributor. In other words, I would need fifty distributors to sell my moonshine nationwide.

I locked down a good distributor right away in Florida, one of the biggest state markets. That was huge. I needed North Carolina, though, and in North Carolina, the situation was . . . complicated. North Carolina didn't allow liquor sales in super-markets, warehouse stores, or independent liquor stores. Only one entity in the state was allowed to sell bottled alcohol to the public: the Alcoholic Beverage Control Commission. The bottles were sold through licensed Alcoholic Beverage Control (ABC) stores.

I needed to get the approval of the state commission, in other words, before I could get a distributor, because no distributor would represent Troy & Sons in North Carolina if my moonshine couldn't be sold there. So I was completely at the board's mercy. A rejection, or even a delay, meant a total business failure. No wonder so many small producers like me still sold their bottles out of the trunk of their car.

The ABC board approval process wasn't a tasting. The board was going to evaluate my entire company, from packaging to quality control to warehouse structure, before agreeing to bring my products into their system. They wanted to taste my moonshine, but they wanted it presented in my shipping boxes and poured out of the actual bottles their stores would be selling, complete with labels.

Preparing for the evaluation was an exhausting process, but Oscar and Pat helped me immensely. Pat advised me on business structure, introducing me to cost accounting and warehouse management programs I never knew I needed and budgeting systems that seemed mind-bogglingly specific. They had to be. Liquor producers are required by law to track *everything*.

Oscar advised me on my presentation. Beer distribution in North Carolina was less strict—beer could be sold in supermarkets as well as ABC stores—but he had dealt with the ABC system for twenty years. He knew some of the board members, and he attended some of the early meetings. He was mostly there for moral support. I had to be the one to sell Troy & Sons, and sell it I did.

I had been thinking of my pitch since the day I asked Forrest Jarrett for the name of an honest-to-goodness moonshiner. I'd been refining that pitch for a year, since it was an integral part of the Troy & Sons brand. I had screen grabs from my in-progress website, sample brochures, media pitches, mock-ups of "shelf talkers" that stores could put beside my bottles to lure customers. They all rested on the three things that made my product unique:

1. It was a traditional moonshine, made in a heritage pre-sugar style and distilled using methods I'd learned from real moonshiners.
2. It was made with top-quality ingredients, like heirloom Crooked Creek corn.
3. I was the first woman to legally distill hard spirits in North Carolina since Prohibition (emphasis on "legally") and the first woman in America to found a whiskey distillery in modern times.

It was a good pitch, not only because it was interesting, but because it was true. I was sure I'd nailed the marketing and business aspects, but the ABC board still needed to taste the product. I had a feeling the bar wasn't too high, considering the nutmeg-flavored swill they were currently selling as "moonshine," but I held my breath nonetheless.

They liked it.

I got my approval at the end of winter, when the snow was melting into slush and the daffodils, those early harbingers of the lovely Southern spring, were erupting into bloom. Any hope that warm weather would see a rebound in the real estate market in rural Buncombe County was dashed, though, as investors dumped properties for pennies on the dollar. There weren't enough buyers, and speculators were circling with rock-bottom offers. We weren't making anything off Whisper Mountain, but we had people living there, so we had to keep the property in good working order. The resident dues barely paid to mow the grass, much less maintain the trails and community center. At that moment, Whisper Mountain was a white elephant, eating us out of our house and home.

The bank wasn't helping. When they rejected a second offer for our house that spring, Charlie and I knew things had to change. A friend gave us the name of a lawyer.

"You have to stop paying your mortgage," the lawyer said. "As long as they are making money every month, the bank has no incentive to accept a short sale."

I was appalled. "Won't they foreclose?"

I had visions of the boys in their wheelchairs on the curb, beside a sad pile of our possessions. And I admit, in my nightmare, the neighbors were looking on and shaking their heads at what a terrible mother I'd been, off in the country making moonshine while my boys' lives fell apart.

"They might," the lawyer said, "but it will be two or three years. The bank is flooded with delinquent mortgages. It will take forever to get around to you."

We had never missed a payment on anything, ever. But this time, Charlie looked at me and kind of shrugged. He didn't like it, but maybe it was a bullet we had to bite. I shook my head. I wasn't ready.

I sent Charlie to Germany on behalf of Asheville Distilling. The distillery was an anthill of activity, with workers rushing to strip the walls back to their concrete blocks and punching holes in the brick exterior for windows. I needed to know not only that my distilling equipment would be ready on time, but that it would be right. The Kothe system included two nineteen-foot stainless steel distillation tower columns, each containing six interior metal plates about a foot apart and round submarine windows so you could see what was happening inside. The vapor from the heated mash would condense on the bottom of each metal plate—whiskey beading on metal is more exciting when viewed through a submarine window, right?—and then revaporize in the hot tower before rising to the next plate, where the same thing would occur. Since there were two towers, this meant each batch of moonshine was vaporized and condensed—"distilled"—twelve times. Twelve distillations was ideal for a pure product. It was also ten more than I'd ever been able to achieve before.

In addition to the tower columns, there was a bulbous pot still, five feet tall at the base with a four-foot copper neck at the top; three stainless mash fermentation tanks so big you needed a ladder to look into them; and a vapor chamber suspended so high no one could touch it from the ground. A good thing, since it was scalding hot during distillation. Together, the seven enormous parts took up thirty square meters of floor space, and they had dozens of gauges and valves that needed to be checked and rechecked during the distillation process.

Charlie came back from Germany excited. The Kothe factory was pristine, he said. The workers were highly skilled. The work was precise. The machine was beautiful. He didn't mean visually appealing, although it was. He meant fantastically engineered. He had run distillations under the company's supervision, and even though the test whiskey wasn't our recipe, the product was crisp and clear.

"You're going to love it, Troy," he said.

When it arrived.

In three months.

"Well, make sure you have this distillery ready," I told him, looking around at the half-finished space.

He smiled. "Yes, boss."

I didn't like it when Charlie called me that. I mean, it was true. We weren't partners. I was the boss. But I wanted a team.

I wanted Charlie and me to be two chiefs, in charge of our own realms, like it should have been at Whisper Mountain.

So I just nodded to him and went back to my home office to prepare for the North Carolina ABC convention, a twice-yearly gathering of ABC store managers that could make or break the company. I had my approval, so North Carolina ABC stores were allowed to buy my moonshine. At the convention, I had to convince the store owners they should.

I had my marketing material. I had my sample bottles and labels. I had John McEntire to charm everyone with his low-key personality and "aw shucks" stories. He and I had gone on several trips together that spring, including to Woodford Reserve outside Lexington, Kentucky, for a media event with foreign writers. I remember John handing a sample of Troy & Sons Platinum to a Japanese reporter, the man trying it, and then the two of them bowing to each other twenty times, not saying a word.

"Well, I don't have any idea what that meant," John said with a laugh, "but I guess it was all right."

John was going to be more in his element with the North Carolina store owners, but I knew I still needed a personal pitch. This wasn't just about being the world's most successful moonshine. That was a small market. If any liquor could get women to give up their Russian vodka for American spirits, I was confident it was Troy & Sons heirloom 'shine.

Could I convince these buyers? I could say until I was blue in the face, "Troy & Sons will be the next Tito's"—a handcrafted vodka out of Austin, Texas, that had smashed Stolichnaya, Absolut, and other lazy, bloated brands—but did I have a plan to make that happen?

And did my moonshine deliver?

I was so nervous leading up to the event, John McEntire

had to talk me down. "Well, law, Troy," he said, "it's just a meeting." John's attitude was that we'd done our best and should be proud, whatever happened. He wasn't worried, partially because I don't think he particularly cared about making money. He just enjoyed the ride.

I wasn't like that at all. I'd put two years into this moonshine, and it was the pure heart—and only the pure heart—of my process. I was confident the buyers would like it, because you have to be confident to sell, but I knew how success worked. Success wasn't making something good and sitting back. Success was hard work. It was sell, sell, sell. If I didn't nail this meeting, I'd never get another round of funding. I'd never create a successful brand. I wouldn't make it to the end of the year. So I walked into the Grove Park Inn on shaky knees, ready to force Troy & Sons down these old boys' throats if I had to.

I didn't have to. Just about every person who tasted my moonshine looked up in surprise and said the same thing:

This is moonshine?

This is from a North Carolina company?

This was made by a woman?

The ABC store managers, who were mostly middle-aged men, looked me up and down, and I knew what they were thinking. *This was made by a woman* like you? Middle-aged. Suburban. Blond. Mom. And yet there was no denying the quality of the product.

It was delicious.

I came away with dozens of orders, and dozens of promises to order in July, when my distillery was officially up and running. *Call me. I'll buy. I promise.* I didn't know if they all intended to buy or not, but I knew one thing: I'd call them back. And I wouldn't stop calling until they did.

"Well, law," John said as we packed the last of our things

and headed out. "I do believe we're going to be all right."

A few weeks later, my personal money ran out, and on the advice of a financial consultant, Charlie and I stopped making the mortgage payments on our house. It felt like failure, but I'd be shipping my moonshine in July, with a three-month float for the buyers to pay. That meant I'd start making money in October. It was already April. As long as the bank didn't foreclose on our house in the next six months—and the financial advisor believed there was no chance of that—we'd be fine.

I suspect you can guess how that turned out.

CHAPTER 28

A HUNDRED RUNS

The bank notified us of their intention to foreclose in late May. "I don't know," the attorney said, shrugging, when I confronted him. "I'm surprised."

"You promised."

"I didn't promise. I said it wasn't likely."

I hated him. Sitting in his office, seeing what looked like fake concern on his face, I hated him. And I hated myself for listening to him. When has anything good come out of refusing to fulfill your obligations? I thought stopping my mortgage payments was the only way to get the bank to take a low offer seriously, but I knew it wasn't right. It was cutting a corner. It was cheating. What did I expect?

"You're not out of the house yet. There's a public hearing."

Public! Oh God. I'm launching a business.

"We can push that back. Probably. You have weeks . . . No, I meant months. Probably."

Meanwhile, my plant manager (and husband) was increasingly on edge. The Kothe was scheduled to arrive soon, and he'd been frustrated by a lack of communication for months. If he made a request, the Germans always replied, "We'll take care of it."

"How?"

"We'll take care of it."

When he asked about a drain, the Germans e-mailed back, "We will put it here," with arrows pointing to the base of the tower.

"Where is here exactly?"

"On the side."

"I need the measurements."

"You don't need the measurements."

Charlie came into my home office once, while I was trying to put together an investor prospectus. Through a friend, Troy & Sons had been invited to cosponsor a party for the Courage Campaign, a progressive organization in California. I'd flown to Los Angeles alone for the event, only to find that the other alcohol sponsor, to my shock, had hired five gorgeous models to serve their drinks and talk up their new vodka line. If that's what it took, I realized, I was in trouble. My seed money was just . . . seeds. I was going to need another round of financing to cover marketing and distribution expenses, and this time I would need a Pat Whalen–style presentation. So while I was drowning in ABC marketing presentations, I was also drowning in monthly overhead projections, typical profit margins in the whiskey business compared to my anticipated profit margin, and other calculations I found next to impossible to make.

Oh Lord, I thought more than once, *get me back to my shack at Peaceful Valley!*

Charlie didn't notice my stress, maybe because I was always

stressed. "I asked the Germans how long the main electric cord would be," he said. "Do you know what they said? 'Long enough.'"

He paused. *Get to the point, Charlie.*

"They don't know where the outlet is! The electrician hasn't even placed it yet. How can they know it will be long enough?"

Deal with it, Charlie. Just deal with it. Can't you see I have a thousand Post-it notes on the walls, not to mention the ones that have fallen on the floor and are sticking to my shoes?

I was up to my neck in budgeting and regulation compliance.

I had to track orders, for both moonshine and supplies.

The warehouse was nearing completion, so I had to order pallets and the plastic to wrap large shipments, and we'd need a forklift to carry heavy pallets, and I had to decide if I was going to buy or rent the forklift, and either way, I needed to find a place for that unanticipated expense in the budget.

And for Lord's sake, we needed the Kothe still, so that I could make moonshine to pay for it all.

The still finally arrived near the end of May, with a team of German installers. Charlie was there to meet them, with our new distilling assistant and warehouse manager, whom I'd hired away from the Apple Store in the mall. The man had no distilling experience, but we got to talking, and he teared up as he told me about his special needs twin sister, who had died the year before. I thought, *This guy will understand me. He will care.*

(He can also help me with any computer problems.)

Charlie and our new hire worked around the clock, making sure everything in the Kothe system was fitting together. I watched my husband guide the installation from our half-completed office overlooking the floor, the gleaming metal machinery slowly filling our empty concrete space. Charlie was fifty-five, but he was still the most handsome man I'd ever met. Tall. Chiseled. Hardly a gray hair on his head. I didn't have a gray hair either, but I was working hard to maintain my blond, if you know what I mean. My husband kept it natural. He had a genuine goodness in his soul.

He looked up, almost as if he could sense me watching. He smiled. I can never resist Charlie's smile. "Well, what do you know?" he yelled up to me.

He held up an electrical cord. He'd never been able to get the measurements from the Germans. Now that it was finally here . . . it was long enough. In fact, it was practically perfect.

"Let's make some moonshine," I said.

We slowed everything down. We had been sprinting for months, but now we had to take our time, because everything rested on getting the whiskey right on the new still. It would take, by my estimation, one hundred distillations before I was confident he could nail the pure heart every time. That was a full summer, since an industrial distillation took ten to twelve hours.

We'd best get started.

I called John McEntire and asked if he could give me another one hundred days. John had always been an early riser, so he had no problem coming in at daybreak to start the distillation process. Charlie arrived about nine to take over, training the new assistant as he worked. I spent the morning putting out fires at home (my office wasn't ready at the distillery, and I'm not sure it could have taken all those Post-it notes anyway), then overseeing the distillation in the afternoon. Marshall and Coulton stayed home with my mother. The distillery was too hot and noisy for them. But Luke often accompanied me to do odd jobs. He loved the work. During the school year, he played football and lacrosse. He told me lugging fifty-pound bags of

Crooked Creek corn was the best workout he'd ever done.

For the first twenty runs (about three weeks), we recorded the temperature, pressure, and other variables every five minutes, so that we could examine our process. We opened the valves to taste and smell the whiskey fifteen times to find the front edge of the heart, and another fifteen to find the back. Everything was written down and analyzed, including the flavor and purity of each distillation. In a way, it was like John and me back in the shed at Pleasant Valley Farm honing our craft, except on a much bigger scale and with twice the team.

It was an expensive and time-consuming process. Each distillation could fill a hundred bottles. When we hit a good one, I'd bottle it and drive around Asheville, visiting restaurants and bars. Other runs weren't up to my standards, and we had to throw them out. During one distillation, a tank suddenly dented. It felt like that violent explosion ripped the heart right out of my chest. What now?! It turned out someone had forgotten to open a valve; a pressure buildup caused the collapse. We banged out the dent, threw that batch away, and kept going. A week later, someone forgot to flush a tank clean. We threw that batch away, too.

During one run, we got twice as much heart as usual. I thought we'd stumbled on a breakthrough. But when we tasted it, the whiskey was only half as good.

"You never get something for nothing," said Oscar, who was passing through.

It was during the second set of twenty runs, when we'd dropped our measurements down to every ten minutes, that the odor became overpowering.

"What stinks?" I said when I arrived after lunch. "For God's sakes, Charlie, it smells like something died."

We scoured the distillery, but everything was clean and in

working order. I was militant about keeping everything clean.

"Something probably did die," Charlie said. "It's outside."

I thought it might be Highland Brewing. Their new tasting room was a roaring success. Crowds were gathering on weekends, and the formerly ratty old warehouse complex had become a hip Asheville destination. We had encouraged them to build a nice deck that stretched from their tasting room to ours (not yet open, sadly), and now they were clearing the back of the property to create a grassy picnic area. Maybe they'd run over a badger or something.

The next day, I realized the problem was us. Our main mash disposal pipe wasn't part of the county waste system, as we had thought. It simply went a few hundred yards into the poison ivy and dumped the used mash into a retention area, where it had turned into a lake of rotting liquid corn.

Charlie and his assistant cleared the fetid lake before it choked someone to death. Then I went back to my old Peaceful Valley Farm solution and found a farmer with enough hogs to eat all our used mash. We never should have dumped the waste into a pipe in the first place. Running a business with a pure heart meant best practices, always. No waste. No shortcuts.

My only break that summer, in fact, was on Sundays. On Sundays, I searched for a new place to live. Apartments had proven inadequate, because of the boys' special needs, so I tracked "for sale by owner" notices in the newspaper, then plotted an afternoon route to hit every open house I could. I knew I couldn't get a loan from a bank. Negotiating an unconventional deal directly with a desperate seller was my only chance.

I wanted to take Luke with me, but he wasn't interested. He was less than two years from high school graduation. He was already thinking about moving on.

I took Marshall instead. I resisted at first, since I could move faster on my own, but Marshall insisted. He wanted to be involved. He wanted to spend time with his mother. He was lonely without me, I suppose, although when I apologized for being away so much he simply banged on his alphabet board: "Love you."

Marshall helped me immensely, because he was so calm, not just in appearance—that was locked in by his physical limitations—but in his words. When his brother was dying, Marshall had written, "Good Mama, Coulton isn't leaving us." He didn't know that, of course, but Marshall always believed God was looking out for those with honest hearts. He said the same to me now, when I asked if he would be sad to leave our house.

"No," he wrote. "We will definitely room with love."

"That was a good place for listening," he wrote one afternoon, after we visited a house outside Asheville. It sat on a country road, with a view of a mountain. I had felt it, too. It was the right place for my boys. We put together an offer. It was unconventional, but I believed it would work for everyone. It didn't.

I was crushed when we didn't get the house. Marshall wasn't disappointed, even for a moment.

"That could be Taccirring," he wrote after visiting another house we weren't able to buy.

When Marshall was a child, he had created the name "Taccirring" for my parents' ranch, a word pronounced with a soft C. When I asked what it meant, he wrote, "Taccirring creates a gorgeous word that is beautiful. Marshall can believe Taccirring has to be a quietly nice said word. Love works willingly there at Taccirring."

To Marshall, "Taccirring" referred to any place that brought him peace. A place that touched his soul. A good place for listening and teaching. For Marshall, "Taccirring" meant home.

Marshall trusted that I would find our Taccirring and "room with love." He trusted me to take care of him. "Love kills fear," he had once written, something I never forgot. Marshall must have feared, especially as his mind began to understand the limits of his body. He must have been terrified. But he had learned love, and he had learned to have faith in me.

I wanted to reward that faith. I wanted to believe we'd find our Taccirring before it was too late. But I was staring at a mountain, and I couldn't quite find his strength.

CHAPTER 29

IT COMES TOGETHER

The full run of bottles arrived from Mexico about the time I received the notice for my public foreclosure hearing. If I couldn't convince the court to let me stay in my home until a sale was worked out, my family and I would be out on the street. I needed to find a place to live. I needed to make arrangements for the boys' care. I needed to get my moonshine to market so I could start making money. I needed to figure out how to use the piece of equipment that filled the bottles with exactly 750 ml of moonshine, because the government was going to make darn sure I wasn't one tenth of a milliliter off.

It only took ten or twelve bottles to realize there was a problem. The bottles had the same amount of liquor in them, but they didn't look the same, because the moonshine came up to different levels.

"The interiors of the bottles are inconsistent," Charlie said.

I called the bottle manufacturer. I told them the shipment

wasn't acceptable. I couldn't put moonshine bottles on the shelves that looked like they'd been filled with a rusty funnel in the backwoods somewhere.

There was a long argument, with lots of excuses and shrugs—"That's not such a problem. Why didn't you mention that when you checked the samples in Mexico? We've sold to blah, blah, and so-and-so and they didn't have any problems."

I didn't care who they'd sold to. I had to have my bottles right. Eventually they agreed to replace the order. It would take a few weeks, but I didn't have a choice. It was only June. I could still make my July on-sale deadline if everything worked out right.

But when the new bottles came, the corks wouldn't fit. They were slipping down into the neck, leading to another twenty thousand rounds of excuses and finger pointing. The cork people said the necks were too big. The bottle people said the corks were too small.

No, the inside of the bottle's neck was supposed to be sloped at a certain angle to hold the cork, but it wasn't. There was a design flaw.

There was no design flaw. The stoppers were made of the wrong kind of cork.

I got the corks fixed. Or maybe it was the bottles; I can't remember. June was dying, and it was clear I wasn't going to make my July deadline.

That's okay, Troy. That's fine. The moonshine coming out of the new distilling equipment is perfect, just the way you want it. If we get it on sale by August, no customers will cancel, and the company will still get paid in October.

Of course in the real world, October wasn't soon enough, since my foreclosure hearing was September 1. Did I mention

I wanted to kill my lawyer? I mean, I wanted to strangle him with my bare hands.

Then we had a problem with the labels.

Well, not the labels themselves. They were perfect. The problem was the machine I'd purchased to apply my beautiful labels to the bottles. It was the second-most expensive thing in the distillery, after the Kothe still. A company representative came to install it. He demonstrated how to use it. Load the labels. Place the bottle. The machine affixed both labels, front and back.

"See," he said happily, before the smile dropped off his face. The labels weren't in the right place. They were crooked. And they were different on every bottle.

The company representative adjusted the machine. He tried again. Adjusted. Tried again.

"It's not our machine," he said. "It's your bottles."

I exploded. I didn't want to hear another word about the bottles. The bottles were fine, they were *what we had,* and I didn't want to waste any more time watching two companies argue with each other over who was responsible for ruining my business and throwing my children out on the street. I needed these labels applied correctly, and I needed them applied now.

I called the representative's boss. I spoke to that guy's boss, and on up the ladder. I'd had enough. I was screaming.

"It's the bottles."

"It's not the flippin' bottles! It's your machine, and I paid good money for it, and it's destroying my business, and I don't want to hear any excuses."

I don't think I'd ever lost control like that before. I was furious. I was under stress. I was tired. I had been up all night, every night, with worry, with Coulton banging, and I didn't want to hear from any more men who seemed perfectly fine foisting their failures onto me.

I wasn't going to pay for the machine. I wasn't going to pay a penny until it was working, and I expected it to be working *right now*.

Fine, they said. The representative packed up the automatic labeler and took it away.

Great. Good. Whatever. The machine was expensive anyway.

I called my friends and business acquaintances. I told them it was an emergency and I needed their help. More than a dozen people came. John McEntire was there. My sister was there. My friends from the neighborhood and school sporting events were there. Luke came with a few of his teenage buddies, who were better workers than us adults. Oscar Wong stopped by, as did Karen Ramshaw, Pat Whalen's wife. Charlie was there, of course, at my side as he'd been for the past nine months. Together, laughing and fumbling, we filled and hand-labeled hundreds of Troy & Sons moonshine bottles, front and back, then hand-wrote the batch number on each label.

It must have been a sight. I had twelve-foot gleaming towers and mash cookers the size of Cadillacs. I had a tank suspended fifteen feet off the ground, a hundred yards of thin glistening pipework bending in every direction, and a back wall stacked five rows high with iron-bound wooden barrels, their tops stamped T & S. The huge clerestory windows for venting vapors were propped open twenty feet up along the top of the outside wall, and the sunlight poured through them at sharp angles, throwing the jagged shadows of my still across the concrete floor while my moonshine condensed in the submarine windows with a quiet sloshing, like the hum of an ultra-quiet washing machine. All that industrial muscle, all that top-of-the-line German ingenuity it had taken me years to acquire, and in my time of greatest need the work was being done by volunteer women and teenagers, scurrying across the floor in all directions and turning themselves around trying to figure out where to go.

That was my summer of family. Or if that word doesn't feel right, it was the summer of the family I had built for myself in Asheville. The label fiasco was the moment I realized all the seeds I'd planted in my life, accidentally and otherwise, would come back to me as trees. There was so much to do in the final weeks before taking Troy & Sons to market. We had to hand-fold shipping boxes. We had to put bottles into those boxes. We had to haul bags of Crooked Creek corn, stack pallets, move boxes that were in the way, clean up, roll empty barrels waiting to age whiskey into their racks, hose down the concrete floor, mark inventory that was spoken for (I'm too old to trust computers without a clipboard backup), and store inventory that was waiting for a buyer, and that doesn't even include more daily problems than you can think of, from losing the forklift key to making sure Highland Brewing would give us access to their bathroom, since we didn't have a bathroom of our own.

There was always someone to help. Every time I hit a snag, it felt like there was another friend walking in the door to lend a hand. Whenever a problem arose, there was always someone I could call. Even Forrest Jarrett, who was long past the age of manual labor, came by once or twice to lighten the mood with his comically oversized personality, and of course to pocket a few bottles he could pet 'n' poke around Buncombe County to spread the word. Forrest Jarrett always seemed to know when something good was in the offing.

The finished bottles, I have to say, looked fantastic. Slim at the bottom and wide at shoulder (like my man!), with a thick base for stability and "Troy & Sons" rising from the glass. Gentle curves. Crisp labels. Smooth clear moonshine, filled exactly to the point where the neck of the bottle rose elegantly toward the cork. The boxes were printed with the Troy & Sons crest and held six bottles each. When I held the first box in my hands, I couldn't quite believe what I'd accomplished. The moonshine was heavy. It was substantial. It was real. And it was legal for me to sell it.

I took four boxes from the first run of fully labeled and bottled Troy & Sons moonshine and put them in my trunk. I planned to drive to a few restaurants that were supporting us to show them the finished product. There is nothing better than a personal touch, after all, and I wanted to make sure I handed each chef and bartender their first official bottle of Troy & Sons Platinum heirloom moonshine.

I'd been driving maybe ten minutes when I heard a loud pop, like a starter's pistol. It startled me so bad, I swerved off the road, worried that I'd blown my engine.

Pop. Pop-pop, pop. I sat behind the wheel in a daze, not sure what was going on, but feeling each pistol shot.

I opened the door, slowly walked around the car, and popped the trunk. It was late August, and it was hot, especially along the shoulder of the road.

As I stared into the trunk, I started laughing. I laugh when I tell the story today, because it's genuinely funny, but at the time, I felt just as much like crying. After all the struggles, all the misfires, and all the help . . . the corks weren't tight enough in the bottles. The heat was causing a buildup of pressure and sending them flying around my trunk like the corks from nice champagne on New Year's Eve.

I happened to be near the Biltmore Estate, where I knew the beverage manager. I rushed over to ask his advice. He suggested adding the wire mesh that held corks on champagne bottles.

I didn't want to do it. I had resisted the idea of covering the corks during the earlier cork/bottle debacles, because I wanted my package clean and beautiful. Everything had to be right. Everything.

But everything wasn't right.

I could live with the wire mesh. I guess.

So I spent a Saturday talking with wire mesh dealers. I spent Sunday looking for a new home for my family. Neither was successful. We couldn't afford any of the houses; the wire mesh didn't come in large enough sizes to fit on our wide-necked bottles.

I decided, reluctantly, to wrap the tops in clear plastic. It was the only way to get my product to market quickly and safely. I could afford a short delay, but not a bottle-based disaster. My corks firing off in a hot ABC warehouse would destroy my business forever. An ugly piece of plastic was far better, but even that solution involved days of hunting down a source and practicing with the heat gun that would melt the plastic tightly around the bottle.

It didn't look bad. Honestly, you barely noticed the plastic.

Honestly, now that I thought of it, I was lucky the corks had exploded in the trunk of my car instead of in some poor sucker's face.

Honestly, I was just plain lucky. Lucky to have dedicated people behind me, especially Charlie. Lucky to have good friends who not only lent a hand when I needed them most, but who had seen the public notice of my foreclosure hearing and didn't hate me for it, as I'd feared. In fact, they did quite the opposite. They comforted me. They knew I was frantically looking for an affordable place to live, and several offered to let our family stay with them. I was grateful for the offers, but Marshall had requirements, and Coulton was loud. All day.

Every night. I couldn't put my friends through that. Still, I was touched by the offers.

Karen Ramshaw was one of those friends who sensed my frustration. Or more accurately, my *fear*. She offered to rent us an apartment she had been holding open in a building she and Pat had renovated downtown. Charlie and I went to see it with her on August 31, 2011. It was a Wednesday, and it was my last chance. The foreclosure hearing was the next morning.

I knew immediately the apartment wouldn't work. The doorways were too narrow for the boys' wheelchairs. The hallway corners were too tight. The bathroom too small. I couldn't afford the rent anyway.

I hugged her and said I loved her. Then Charlie and I drove home in silence. The boys were waiting for us, as they always were. Marshall and Coulton were incapable of doing anything but waiting until someone reached out to them. I reached out to hug them, to love them, but what good would that do now?

I went to my bedroom. I went into the walk-in closet, where I had been going for months to scream. Charlie found me fifteen minutes later in the corner.

"I can't, Charlie . . . I can't . . ."

I was in a fetal position, with my arms wrapped around my knees. Charlie tried to pull my arms apart, but he couldn't. My muscles were locked. I had been crying so hard, my body had shut down.

"I can't move. Charlie . . . I can't breathe."

Once again, an ambulance was called to the Ball home. This time, it was for me.

It was a panic attack, the EMTs said as they slowly coaxed me out of my body lock. I had hyperventilated and collapsed from exhaustion and stress. They gave me fluids and medicine, then helped me to my bed. I just needed time, they said. I needed to relax and breathe.

I didn't have time. I couldn't relax. The foreclosure hearing was the next morning. I had run as far as I could, as fast as I could, but I hadn't made it. Now I had nowhere to go and nothing left to do.

The next day, Charlie and I waited in the hearing room, not saying a word to each other. I was so sore, I could barely stand. Every muscle in my body hurt. I had clenched my jaw so hard for so long that my teeth were still throbbing. I don't know how long I sat there, in pain, with Charlie beside me, but it seemed like an eternity. Finally the judge came in. The hearing had been canceled. It would be rescheduled.

"What happened?" I asked.

The bank hadn't bothered to show up.

A month later, the Asheville Distilling Company shipped its first full pallet of Troy & Sons Platinum heirloom moonshine.

CHAPTER 30

SELL, SELL, SELL

Just like my friends had pulled together for me, Asheville came out to support us, in its own low-key way. We didn't have an official opening. There was no symbolic breaking of bottles against the still, as if we were launching a yacht. No YouTube video. We didn't even throw a party. I don't like parties. For two decades, I didn't have the freedom to attend them, so I fell out of the habit. I hadn't celebrated my birthday or anniversary with anything more than an ice-cream cone since the Reagan presidency.

But when we opened our tasting room doors on Friday and Saturday nights, people came. Highland Brewing had a couple food trucks that parked next to their picnic lawn, and young people and families often gathered for free weekend concerts. It almost killed me that we couldn't sell moonshine out of our tasting room, especially since Highland Brewing had turned their tasting room into one of the area's most successful beer bars. But the ABC commission was aggressive in protecting its monopoly, and the state laws were clear: we couldn't sell a drop.

We found strong support, though, in Asheville's famous independent restaurants. My first commercial sale was to Joe Scully, the chef and owner of Corner Kitchen, the Asheville favorite in Biltmore Village where Charlie and I had eaten our first local meal. Joe was from New Jersey, but he was an FOF: Friend of Forrest. A while back, the two of them had cooked up a wild-game charity dinner featuring local animals hunted by Forrest and "his boys." Today, you can't get a ticket unless you're connected, the event is so popular, but at the original Wild Game Dinner, I was the only woman. Joe was a big supporter of local businesses, and once his staff tasted my moonshine (Joe doesn't touch alcohol), he was one of my best advocates. He ordered so early he had to wait for Troy & Sons to be available, since the ABC distribution network wasn't in nearly as much of a hurry as I was.

Katie Button, a young female chef who had just moved to Asheville, was another early supporter. She was opening a Spanish restaurant named Cúrate, and we hit it off over female entrepreneurship, the evolution of culinary and beverage traditions, and the joy (and challenges) of working with your husband.

My sister Trish helped us get into the Biltmore Estate's numerous restaurants and bars.

Our big coming out, though, was the Asheville Wine & Food Festival, a showcase for local gourmet products and nationally renowned chefs. It was a perfect launch for Troy & Sons, since it took place in the fall and catered to our core market. I worked on signage, brochures, and my booth for months. I tested cocktail recipes with my sister and a few friends—a fun part of the job, I admit—and created a recipe booklet for the festival. It included information on the company and John McEntire's heirloom corn, and recipes for our three favorite concoctions: the TNT (Troy 'n' Tonic), the TLC (Troy-Lime-Cola), and the Son-Shine Margarita. They were versions of classic cocktails, but they pointed toward something important. Troy & Sons moonshine wasn't just a replacement for whiskey; it was an ideal substitute for the gin, vodka, and tequila traditionally used in those drinks.

I put together an all-female festival team of my sisters and friends, including two who flew in from Texas for the weekend. It was work, sure, but it was so much fun. The festival was a thousand-person party, and we were the only distiller. We served sample cups of moonshine and a fruit punch called the Shooting Star, a tribute to the accidental cocktail I'd served when Forrest Jarrett gave me my first batch of keeper 'shine and to that old Asheville classic from the 1930s, twenty-four-hour punch.

I don't think anyone expected a bunch of middle-aged women (who didn't feel middle-aged at all) to be schlepping moonshine, and I know they weren't expecting our moonshine cocktail to be so delicious. People were coming back for fourths and fifths of our mini-cups, especially women. We were laughing and dancing, having a great time. And we were selling my brand—local, traditional, delicious, female, and fun—to every foodie and restaurant owner in the region.

Soon after, Tupelo Honey, the city's most popular restaurant, especially with tourists, added Troy & Sons cocktails to its "recommended" menu. I'd learned pretty quickly the only way to move bulk in a bar or restaurant was to be in their well (the cheap option the bartender grabbed whenever someone ordered a generic whiskey or vodka) or to be recommended.

So being Tupelo Honey's go-to whiskey was a big deal for us. It felt like, at least in Asheville, we'd arrived.

I remember Pat Whalen shaking his head and laughing at one of our last mentor sessions. Pat had never given me any contacts at the restaurants and bars he'd helped finance. That wasn't his style. He worked behind the scenes, earning his entire dollar. He was in touch with people, though, and I guess word was getting back to him that I was a hard-driving, hard-selling SOB.

"I didn't think you had it in you, Troy," Pat said. "Most people don't. But you are a force of nature."

Of course, selling individual restaurants and bars could only take us so far, as I learned when I went to Miami with sample bottles on the advice of my Florida distributor. I had a great event for bar managers hosted by a restaurant sommelier in Miami Beach who loved my moonshine. We really hit it off, as only two women in a man's business can. She placed a big order. Eight bottles. A bunch of bars also placed orders . . . for three or four bottles apiece. At that pace, I realized, I was going to have to sell thousands of accounts.

Unfortunately, I was hitting snags on my home ground. Asheville was my base and most important market, but it was small. I needed the rest of North Carolina to embrace us, and that wasn't happening. I'd shipped a thousand bottles to ABC stores around the state, but they weren't moving off the shelves. There just wasn't any reason for customers in, say, Wilmington or Fayetteville to buy Troy & Sons. I didn't have money for advertising or promotions run through my distributor, and the articles that had been written about us were mostly local. If I didn't personally pitch to store owners, we weren't making our numbers.

I'd run into an even bigger problem in Charlotte, by far the state's largest market. One of the ABC store board members there had gone on my website and noticed I had a button for Internet sales. He complained to the state commission, who called and told me Internet sales were illegal in the state of North Carolina. Everything had to go through ABC.

"I'm not selling over the Internet," I said. I was simply offering a link to a liquor store in Florida that had a system for Internet sales.

"Can't do that. Everything has to go through us."

"You do realize you can buy Jack Daniel's on the Internet, right? You sell Jack Daniel's, don't you? Why are you treating us differently?"

"Sorry. Everything has to go through us."

"Then why don't we create a system for Internet sales?"

I thought this was a great solution and that ABC was a reasonable, flexible organization. In fact, I'd already solved one vexing problem with their system. Everything ABC sold had to go through their warehouse in Raleigh, even sales to businesses in Asheville. This was more than inefficient; it was prohibitively expensive, since every pallet of Troy & Sons I sent to their central warehouse (a pallet held 540 bottles) cost me $400 in shipping fees.

When I analyzed the problem, I saw that, since my distillery was less than a mile from the main east-west highway, the ABC trucks were driving the pallets I sent to Raleigh right back past us when they delivered to local stores. What a crazy, stupid system! I was tearing my blond hair out in frustration. Then I realized: the trucks were driving right past us on the way back too, but by then they were empty.

I called the ABC warehouse manager. "Do you mind if I put my moonshine on your empty trucks? I'm a mile out of the way, but I'll cover that cost. Heck, I'll meet you on the side of the road."

It took a few weeks for the idea to work its way through the bureaucracy, but eventually they agreed. In the first month alone, shipping on ABC trucks saved me thousands of dollars. That's nothing to Bacardi, but it was huge for Asheville Distilling. Eventually, the ABC managers turned my empty truck idea into a statewide shipping program, with a small fee. Good for ABC, great for small alcohol producers, just fine for Troy & Sons. We're competitors with every other North Carolina distiller, but we're all in this together.

I thought having the ABC commission run my Internet sales was a great idea. After all, those sales were almost all coming from other states, where I didn't yet have a distributor. That meant more money for ABC. More money for me. More money, in tax revenue, for the state of North Carolina.

The ABC commission didn't see it that way, and neither did the board member in Charlotte. Long story short, that one man got Troy & Sons blackballed in the Charlotte metropolitan area. That's 2.3 million customers, in a state with a population just shy of 10 million. I guess he did it on principle. Maybe. It felt like he did it for spite.

It was becoming increasingly clear that, despite my best efforts, a one-woman sales force and a darn good bottle of moonshine could only go so far. If I'd had the time to grow things organically—generate enough income to hire a second salesperson, use the additional sales to invest in advertising and marketing, then roll that into a contract with a large outside sales force—I could have made it work. I was on the right path. Heck, as the first female whiskey distiller in America, I was blazing that path.

But I didn't have the freedom to slug my way forward, one step at a time. I had a new court date set for my foreclosure hearing, and I had another offer on our house. It was lower than any of the previous offers, but I was determined to make it stick. The bank had to accept a short sale and write off the loss so that Charlie and I could avoid personal bankruptcy, get our financing in order, and get on with our lives. I wasn't going to take no for an answer this time, and I wasn't going to be ignored.

I don't know what changed. It was probably something that had nothing to do with me, just as the bank's decision to force foreclosure had nothing to do with me, my house, or the Asheville market. Luck of the draw? Maybe. I like to think the difference was perseverance. That if you never give up, good things might happen.

We went to court on our foreclosure notice in late October, while the offer was pending. We were determined not to give up or to give in. "We have a buyer," we told the court. "Force the bank to talk to us. Give us time to work it out."

The court agreed and postponed the foreclosure while we negotiated. The bank, legally obligated to make an effort, gave up and accepted the offer. I went to the buyer on hands and knees and begged him for time to find a new place to live. I got lucky. The buyer had placed the first offer on our house, which the bank had rejected the year before. He had come back and bought the house for 30 percent less than he would have paid then. He was thrilled. Even better, he was buying it as a second home, so he didn't need to move in right away. He agreed to lease the house back to us at a reasonable price for the next four months.

I wasn't home free—a funny expression, given the circumstances. Not even close. I had wrangled a better housing arrangement, by far, than I'd anticipated. I'd survived for six months with the foreclosure hanging over my head. I'd opened my distillery and had money coming in. I still had our huge up-front costs to repay before turning a profit, and I still had to find a permanent home for Marshall and Coulton, but I had four months—an entire four months!—and that meant I had room to breathe.

Fortunately, a solution was already within reach. All I had to do was grasp it.

CHAPTER 31

CONNECTIONS

The relationship started in the tasting room, a couple weeks after our launch. Charlie and Luke were giving tastings and tours on weekend evenings, when Ashevillians descended on the lawn outside Highland Brewing to hang out and listen to bands. We had a simple yet elegant space, with two-story-high windows that shone with warm light after sunset and a sparklingly clean stainless steel and copper distilling rig that never failed to impress. We were walk-in friendly, and we always drew a crowd.

It seemed like such a wasted opportunity. Money was tight. If only we could have sold a bottle to the people who liked our samples, instead of sending them to a local ABC store—an extra trip I'm sure most of them never made. If only we could have provided for the people who wanted a keepsake of their trip to Asheville, or who thought, *What the heck, it's right here, moonshine will make an interesting gift for Dad*. A few thousand dollars a month would have given us a nice cushion, and it wouldn't even have dented the statewide demand. But the North Carolina system was against us. It was set up to help the most powerful liquor lobby in the state, the ABC stores, and nobody cared if that hurt local entrepreneurs like me.

Fortunately, on this particular night Charlie was in charge of the tasting room. Luke was a natural tour guide; he's a charming kid with a great smile, and everyone loved him. But Charlie was our expert. He had thrown himself into the daily life of the distillery, and he could talk for hours about our process, our equipment, and our ingredients. In less than a year, my whiskey had become his passion, something I never would have anticipated when he was laughing at my homemade pressure-cooker still and saying I would blow up the house. Now Charlie knew the Kothe system better than I did, which made sense, since his official title was master distiller.

"This is a great moonshine," a man said that evening while sitting in our tasting room after the tour. The other tour members agreed, before slowly drifting away empty-handed as the evening deepened, off to listen to the music on the lawn or to the Highland tasting room, which sold twelve Highland beer varieties on tap. Charlie and the man stayed behind and talked about the company, then slowly drifted over to the Highland tasting room themselves to continue chatting.

"I have a friend who's been looking for investment opportunities," the man said. "Are you interested in something like that?"

"We're preparing a prospectus," Charlie said.

"Don't send it to anyone until you've heard back from me."

Neither of us thought much about it. There's a lot of loose talk in business, and usually nothing comes of it. I had forgotten about the chance meeting, in fact, until we got a call in early November. The caller represented an executive who had been tipped off to Troy & Sons by our friendly tour participant. He had been watching us, and he was impressed. He loved our moonshine, and he loved our business.

November 2011 was a big month for me. That was the month the bank finally accepted the offer on our house in Asheville and I secured another four months of breathing space from the buyer (who has since become a good friend). It was the month Asheville Distilling really started pumping out moonshine, shipping pallets as fast as we could produce them. And it was the month the first national press for Troy & Sons hit newsstands, in the December issue of *Garden & Gun*.

I don't think there could have been a more appropriate match. I was distilling moonshine for women who gardened, and men who hunted, and everybody in between. I was making a product as Southern as the idea that gardens and guns go together like biscuits and gravy, and my life embodied that ethos. My world combined the patient domesticity of the mother of special needs boys with the freewheeling aggression of an entrepreneur. The beginning of the article hinted at that truth:

> Chances are if you met Troy Ball on the street, the last thing you'd think is "moonshiner." But sip the white lightning this energetic businesswoman is whipping up, and you'll most likely get down on your knees and thank the heavens she's found her calling.

Amen!

November ended with Charlie and me driving to Atlanta to meet the potential investor. The drive west and then down through the mountains is quiet. It is nothing but trees and ridges, green in the summer but white in the winter, the bare fingers of the branches near the roads like spiderwebs, the round forms of the trees on the farther mountains like puffs of breath in the freezing air. Last year at Thanksgiving, I'd been hosting Forrest's birthday party and fretting over how to get through the winter. I'd felt hopeful but crushed, wondering if there was a way out of the cul-de-sac Charlie and I seemed to be hurtling into.

I had come a long way since then. I'd built my life and business consistently upward over the course of the year, never daring to stop working or look back at where I'd been. But I was always aware, in the back of my mind, that my financial progress was too slow. Homelessness was looming; the first round of investment cash was dwindling. I had four months, not four years. If I was going to be solvent by spring, I needed this relationship to work.

I brought the prospectus with me to Atlanta. It was full of lawyer-verified numbers and calculations, the kind of written plan I found wasteful and foolish but businessmen like Pat Whalen loved. I didn't talk numbers, though, when I walked into the plush boardroom and found ten executives gathered around a long table. Instead, Charlie and I passed our moonshine to the men—they were all men—and let them taste it. Then I told my story.

I started all the way back in Texas with Marshall and Coulton's health scares, the reason we moved to Asheville. I told them about Forrest Jarrett's pet 'n' pokes and John McEntire's ramshackle farm full of off-kilter sheds. I told them about my research in the archives in Raleigh on pre-Prohibition information, and my long night at the hunting camp in Alabama, and my fourteen months in a boiling-hot-and-then-freezing shack perfecting my craft. I explained why Troy & Sons was different from the sugar-based moonshines that were our competition, and how John McEntire and I had cornered the market on Crooked Creek corn, the best heirloom grain for making whiskey this side of the moon.

I told them I was creating two aged whiskeys, one using a rare heirloom Turkey Red wheat John was growing on his uncle Leroy's farm. I already had barrels aging in the back of my warehouse. They'd be ready in three short years.

"Troy & Sons isn't a moonshine," I told them. "It's my family, and it's my family brand. It stands for tradition, quality, perseverance, love, and care. I'm not making cheap products, and I never will. I'm going to bottle the pure heart of my whiskey. Nothing else. No matter how big we get or how many products we produce, that's what Troy & Sons will be: pure heart. If you're interested in that, I'm interested in hearing what you can provide."

"We're interested," the lead investor said when I finally stopped talking.

The room, he explained, was full of experienced marketers and salespeople from the corporate business world. They were impressed with what I'd done alone, but it was progress by inches, knocking down one door at a time. These men could open a thousand doors at once, because they had contacts I could only dream of. They could distribute Troy & Sons in all fifty states, and they could support their distribution with a million dollars of marketing and advertising. In exchange for a piece of the company, they would immediately provide what it would take me years to build alone: a nationwide presence.

"It will cost you," I said. "This brand is my heart. I won't sell it cheap."

But I already knew that if the money was reasonable, I'd take it. I had to.

I went back to Asheville and tried to forget about the deal. The lawyers were taking over the negotiations, and that meant a long process. The agreement could easily fall through. It was my job to put my head down and continue to build my brand. No matter what happened, I was the heart of Troy & Sons.

One of the first things I did was hire a new employee, Kenn Phillips, even though I didn't need another employee. I had hired two young men since the summer, when my friends had come in to help me lift Troy & Sons off the ground, and we were running lean. Then Kenn sent me an e-mail asking for an unpaid internship. He had taken brewing classes at a local community college, and he wanted experience in the business. Something about his tone made me agree to meet him.

When he came for an interview the next morning, Kenn said straightaway, "Troy, I need to be honest with you about myself."

Kenn had been a police officer in the county sheriff's department for seventeen years. He thought he'd work there for life; then his young niece was murdered. Kenn was single, and the niece was like a daughter to him. He started investigating the case, even though it wasn't his assignment. He was told to back down, but he couldn't let it go. After the investigation ended without an arrest, his life fell apart. He needed to find his niece's killer, and he couldn't stop trying until he had done everything in his power. Eventually he was transferred out of the sheriff's department to the community college, where he taught classes on criminal justice. Slowly he began to put his life back together. But when the recession hit, the criminal justice program was cut to save money, and Kenn found himself out of work.

"I've applied unsuccessfully for one hundred and sixty-seven jobs," he told me, hanging his head. "I know this doesn't pay, but I need something." He paused. "The truth is, I'm living in my Jeep."

I could tell it hurt. I could hear the desperation in his voice, but also his resignation. Kenn had learned to accept what he'd done, along with the consequences.

"I know how you feel," I said. "It probably doesn't look like it, but I nearly landed on the street myself. I know how much it hurts. So if you come back tomorrow morning, I'll give you a job. It won't be much, you'll be at the bottom, but it won't be an internship. It will be a paying position."

Kenn started crying, right there at my desk. The next morning, he was waiting for me in the parking lot, clutching something to his chest. It was a picture of his niece. "I wanted you to see the reason for the choices I made," he said. "She was my life."

I understood. I was living my life for other people, too.

By Christmas, the distillery had settled into a rhythm, and I was thinking past Asheville. If I really was turning over sales and marketing to new partners, that meant I'd be out of the part of the business that had been my original passion, the talent Dad had drilled into me with those Zig Ziglar seminars when I was ten years old. I had secured my largest order yet from the Harrah's casino in Cherokee, North Carolina. The food and beverage manager wanted to pitch Troy & Sons to the national office. That would mean sixteen casinos, with more than a hundred bars and restaurants and millions of annual visitors.

I was opening up distribution in South Carolina and Georgia. I was ramping up sales in Florida. But I wanted more. I wanted an account that wasn't just large but symbolic and grand. I wanted a *victory*. The more I thought about it, the more it became clear that what I really wanted while the company was entirely my own was Disney World.

My Florida distributor said I was crazy. "You have to be on

their supply list," he told me. Fine, we'll get on their supply list.

"You have to know somebody." Then let's meet the right people.

"Disney is for families. They will never, ever, ever sell something called moonshine."

The distributor was right. Disney turned me down multiple times, without so much as hearing my pitch. Dad was with me, though. His spirit was whispering in my ear: *Do you know what you need to do, Troy? Next time we talk, I want to hear you've done it.*

I flew down to Florida in the dead of winter, when the North Carolina mountains were shrouded in fog. I visited every bar and restaurant on the Disney property, giving the managers my card and talking with them about my moonshine. I pitched until I had to drag myself back to my hotel, almost too hoarse to call home and wish my sons good night. I knew nobody was going to bite. Disney was too hierarchical for individual managers to make impromptu decisions. But I was planting seeds, as Dad always said. I was planting seeds.

I returned to North Carolina empty-handed, but by then other plants were starting to bloom. I pitched Troy & Sons to Sean Brock's legendary Charleston restaurant Husk, and they placed an order on the spot. Suddenly, the most respected chef in the Southeast was a supporter.

I opened a dozen new accounts in Asheville, including one of my personal favorite restaurants, Rhubarb.

After hundreds of open houses, Charlie and I found an owner-financed house in Arden, North Carolina, a small town near Asheville. We needed to convert the garage into an accessible ground-floor space for Marshall and Coulton, but otherwise it was move-in ready. This was a place, finally, I could see our family living. I negotiated a good deal that allowed us the flexibility to make the modifications for the boys, and Charlie set to work on the renovations.

Soon after, Charlie and I drove to Atlanta to close the distillery deal. It was a bittersweet day. I was signing away half my company to a group of men I barely knew to secure a sound financial future for my boys. That hurt. But at the same time, it was one of the most triumphant moments of my life. I'd done it. I'd built a business from scratch and mostly on my own. I'd created a brand that stood for something and lived up to my highest ideals. I'd sold a chunk of that brand for a large profit. The money wouldn't make us rich. We'd never get back to where we were before Whisper Mountain. But that wasn't my goal. The money was enough to make my family whole. More importantly, I'd earned every penny. When my life looked bleakest, I'd reached down inside, pulled myself forward, and saved us all.

I signed the contract. I drank a spiderleg to celebrate with my new partner and Charlie, toasting Troy & Sons and our future success. Maybe my new partner could sense a rim of sadness, the gray edge of loss on my happiness, because as I was heading out the door, he grabbed me by the arm.

"The moonshine's good," he said. "I love it. Don't change a thing. But I want you to understand, Troy, that I'm not investing in this company just because of the whiskey. I'm doing it because I believe in you."

TACCIRRING

The call from my distributor about Disney's Wilderness Lodge came out of the blue. Apparently, after my visit, one of the beverage managers had tried making some cocktails with Troy & Sons. He liked the Troy & Sons family story and our commitment to quality. He thought a "Moonshine Margarita" would be a good fit for his rustic hotel theme. It would take a while to get Troy & Sons in the Disney system, but if I was willing to put in the work, the Wilderness Lodge was willing to put my moonshine on its recommended cocktail list on a trial basis.

"I can't believe it," my distributor said. "Troy, I simply cannot believe it. I didn't think we had a chance."

I was in shock. I hung up the phone and turned to Charlie, who was sitting at a desk a few feet from mine in our shared office above the tasting room. "I sold Disney," I said. On my own, with my little independent company and no contacts, I had landed my most coveted account. Not to mention, as a human being and mother, I loved Disney. Who doesn't love Disney? My heart, at that moment, was jumping through my chest.

"Miracles happen," I said.

With hard work and a pure heart, you can make miracles happen.

Or sometimes, if you've lived with a pure heart all your life, they happen on their own. That's what I thought when I received another call out of the blue, this one asking if I was Marshall Ball's mother.

"Yes. Who is this?"

She was calling on behalf of Chris Martin, the lead singer of Coldplay, one of the most popular bands in the world. Chris was a big fan of Marshall's writings, the woman said. He wanted to invite Marshall to his concert in Charlotte as his special guest.

I put the phone down in more shock than when I'd landed the Disney account, and with more joy in my heart. You have to understand, nobody had called for Marshall in years. For a time in the late 1990s, when his book *Kiss of God* was on the bestseller list, Marshall had been an inspiration and a teacher to thousands. He had written a second book. It was published in September 2001, and although I believe the world needed his message of love and acceptance even more because of the tragedy, the book was buried by that terrible day.

Since then, Marshall had been alone. He had been locked in a silent world, on his back or in his wheelchair, with no one to listen to him, or care about him, but his family. He had been thirteen when the whole world heard his words; now he was twenty-eight and forgotten. Or so I had thought, until this young woman told me *Kiss of God* was being studied as a guide to happiness in certain circles in Los Angeles.

"Marshall is loved here," she said.

Charlie, Luke, and I took Marshall to the concert. We pushed him backstage in his wheelchair, as instructed, and found Chris Martin playing a furious game of Ping-Pong. When he was finished, he bent down so that he could look Marshall in the eye while he talked to him. I almost burst into tears. You have to understand, nobody bent down and talked to Marshall with respect like that. Not even my best friends. Not even his brother Luke, who loved Marshall as much as a teenager can love anyone other than himself.

"This is an honor, Marshall," Chris said. "I've been reading your book every day." Marshall tapped his heels furiously together, a signal that he was furiously happy.

They had placed a wooden platform at the back of the floor so that Marshall could see over the crowd from his wheelchair. As I sat there with Marshall and Charlie, waiting for the show to start, I reflected on my life. It hadn't been a short or an easy path, but I'd become a successful entrepreneur, as I'd always wanted. I was a success as a mother. I'd given my family financial security.

Maybe the house in Arden wasn't what I'd always dreamed of. It was the smallest house I'd owned since before Listener's Hill. But I knew now, like I maybe hadn't known before, that my family didn't need something large and beautiful to be happy. We needed wide doors and no stairs, with a big enough bathroom for two special boys and their gear. We needed a place we could live together, for as long as we chose, or until time finally bent us like it does the mightiest oak and our Father called us home.

As Marshall wrote, in a message I placed inside the walls of his new room before they were sealed forever: "Love is sweetly written, teaching the listener to love."

Our love, as my sweet son has always understood, would make the house our Taccirring. Our place to feel peace. Our place to listen and teach each other.

I could see that love when Charlie lifted Marshall gently from his wheelchair and placed our son on his lap. Marshall leaned his head on Charlie's shoulder, his favorite gesture of togetherness. After a while, the lights went down and the arena got dark.

"This one is for my good friend Marshall Ball, who is here tonight," Chris Martin said. The lights came up. The band launched into their hit song "Yellow." The crowd roared. Marshall tapped his heels, safe in Charlie's arms. And as yellow confetti began to fall around us, I began to realize that Taccirring wasn't just a place. It was a feeling, too, a moment in time. It was this moment in time, with Luke and my husband and my son the teacher beside me, and that meant I hadn't needed to go out into the world to find my Taccirring, because I had already found it.

It had been with me all along.

A Whisper from a Mountain

VICTORY IS HERE.

IT GIVES US THAT ROOM

TO QUIETLY TITLE OUR THOUGHTS.

We threw an eighty-fifth-birthday party for Forrest Jarrett at Asheville Distilling in November 2015. We strung paper lanterns above the deck outside and turned the lights up in the tasting room so everyone could see the distilling towers through the windows. The place glowed beneath the dark purple of the Asheville late autumn sky, a warm home against the cold. We hired one of Forrest's favorite bluegrass bands and everyone danced in the barrel room, where it was cozy and warm. Forrest was in fine form, sporting rattlesnake skin on his Stetson and ostrich skin on his boots. I don't see Forrest as much as I used to at Angelwood, but I knew I'd made it when he started introducing me as "my moonshining lady." You're in with the old pistol-toter if he gives you a title, and I guess that's mine.

I don't remember everyone who was there, because there were more than two hundred people. It was my extended family in Asheville and the mountains, all the people who made my story complete. There were Forrest's friends from our breakfast group, including Jerry Rogers, who was having health issues and didn't get out much anymore. There were business supporters who had mentored me over the years. Tons of local chefs and bartenders made an appearance, some after the dinner shift, a few deep in the night to finish off the last moonshine bottles, like true restaurant professionals.

The friends who had helped me during that first busy summer came to bask in the warm glow of the distillery's success. Oscar Wong couldn't make it, but he'd dropped by earlier to help with the preparations, even though he'd sold his interest in the distillery. He was in the process of turning Highland Brewing over to his daughter, and as he put it, his wife wanted him to retire for real this time.

All five of my employees, including Kenn Phillips, took the opportunity to drink the moonshine they spent their days making. I had taken a chance on Kenn, and he had turned out to be one of my most valuable employees. He was willing to do anything I asked, and he'd even started visiting local bars and restaurants on his days off and telling them to carry Troy & Sons whiskey, because Troy & Sons was the right kind of company. I don't pay him for that. When I asked him why he did it, he said, "Because I'll do anything for you, Troy. I'm your guy."

That's pure heart. That's why I'm as loyal to Kenn, and all my employees, as they are to me.

Charlie was there, of course, sitting on the side with Marshall and Coulton, looking as handsome as the day I married him. Luke came home from Western Carolina College, where he was a sophomore trying to figure out life. My sister Trish brought her two sons.

My mother was the only local family member missing. Mom had spent her whole life caring for others, first Dad and her children, then me and the boys. It seemed her lot in life was to be the strength that held others up, the quiet presence at our sides. Every time Charlie and I were somewhere else in this book, it was because Mom was at our home caring for the boys.

Her loyalty reminds me how wrong I was during those years at home with Marshall, Coulton, and Luke, when I felt like a failure because I wasn't following Dad's example. I hadn't strayed. I had never forsaken my upbringing. For those twenty-four years, I had been following Mom's example, and Mom is my hero, too.

I don't have her strength. She was too good at giving, and she seemed so fulfilled in that role. Then one day, soon after we moved to the house in Arden, she announced, "I think it's time for this little bird to leave the nest."

She was in her seventies! No matter. A few weeks later, she moved back to Kerrville, Texas . . . where she promptly rented an apartment and began taking care of her older neighbors. So who's to say it's ever too late to live the life you want?

John McEntire was with me at the distillery, of course, standing in the shadows with his daughter Lindsey, quiet but happy. It was one of the few times my two whiskey guides were ever together. Forrest and John were different types of men, even though they both spent their lives in Appalachia. Maybe it was the difference between growing up east of Asheville (the low mountains) and west (the high), or maybe we're all our own people, no matter where we're from. Forrest would have given me the shirt off his back (stylishly stitched, with an outrageously large collar covering the top of his bolo tie) if I asked, but he was a talker.

John was a doer. He didn't spend much time at Asheville Distilling, but we had a few business ventures going together. I'd convinced him to clear his awful debris pile of a sawmill and replace it with a full-scale corn-grinding operation. John had bartered for two storage silos cheap, and we had enough capacity to grind corn for other growers as well as all my Crooked Creek. Then we'd decided to go in together on heirloom pigs, fed on used Troy & Sons mash. So we had a vertical monopoly on Crooked Creek corn, taking it from seed to feed without anyone else touching it.

We hadn't made much money on these ventures. John liked to say we were "pig poor," but we hadn't lost any money either, and with John McEntire, that felt always like the point. With John, the journey was so much fun, I didn't much worry about the results.

The lack of progress with Troy & Sons was more disappointing. My moonshine was receiving raves, including an "exceptional" rating and gold medal from the Beverage Testing Institute. I had introduced my two aged whiskeys in early 2015 with equal success. My Troy & Sons Oak Reserve, a traditional dark whiskey, received an A (91) from the *Tasting Panel;* my Blonde, a refined light-golden whiskey, received a 95, a rare honor for a young whiskey aged only three years.

It turned out, though, that you can't skip straight from being a local favorite to a national brand. You still need to take the steps to work your way there. Troy & Sons was building market share, but the build was slow. Even in Asheville, the business seemed to be two steps forward and one step back. Joe Scully, my friend from Corner Kitchen, opened a new restaurant called Chestnut. His signature dish was a she-crab soup, topped with Troy & Sons Oak Reserve foam.

My friend Katie Button's restaurant, Cúrate, had taken off. She was barely thirty, and Cúrate was already being hailed as one of the top Spanish-influenced restaurants in the country.

She was selling thousands of her signature cocktail, the Eclipse de Luna, which featured Troy & Sons moonshine.

The Moonshine Margarita, meanwhile, turned out be the number-one-selling cocktail at Disney's Wilderness Lodge. Of course it did. Who could resist a moonshine margarita?

Unfortunately, I'd lost my place on the recommended cocktails list at Tupelo Honey. The original owner had sold out to a businessman, and the bar manager told me I needed to pay $3,000 if I wanted to stay on their drink list. I can't afford to pay every restaurant that serves Troy & Sons, so I had to decline. They stopped pushing cocktails featuring my whiskeys the next week, but we're still on the back bar, and I still love their food.

Maybe that's the kind of thing that caused the disagreements between my new partners and me. Or maybe we simply have different styles. They believed in bulk sales, while I believed in the personal touch. I wanted to market my story and explain what "Troy & Sons" meant. I wanted to be a huge brand, sure, but I also wanted to hold on to the Asheville values that made us special. I mean, if Forrest Jarrett could share his moonshining friends, and John McEntire could share his farm, and Pat Whalen could share his experience for a single dollar, and Charlie at Tomato Jam could share her soul with a hug every day when Coulton was dying and I needed it most . . . who would I be if I refused to pass that love and faith along?

They didn't quite see it that way. They didn't want to sell the "Troy" in Troy & Sons, just the spirit inside. "Don't worry, little lady," they as much as told me. "We're the experts here. We know what we're doing."

So it was only my Asheville friends at the distillery that November night, when I gave Forrest a mini-keg of Troy & Sons Oak Reserve, signed by all the guests. The mini-keg was a novelty item I kept for gifts and decorating, but I knew it was perfect for Forrest. I crossed my fingers and hoped he'd put it in the cabin behind his house, beneath his photographs of Jesse James Bailey and Popcorn Sutton, and next to the bed where his grandmother Polly O'Dell was born and Mama Linda died. If that happened, I'd know I'd made it.

I have made it, actually. Maybe not in the traditional American sense of having millions of dollars and my own reality show—although I have appeared on the show *Moonshiners* several times with my moonshining friend Tim Smith. I've made it in the sense of knowing myself and finding peace with what I've done with my life.

I'll never stop pushing Troy & Sons and our heirloom values, but I have only one major goal left in my life. Marshall wants to create a public Taccirring, a nature preserve with a walking path that he will line with art, music, and his simple but profound thoughts. A place designed with love, where anyone can listen to and learn from the world around them.

I have to do that for Marshall, who has waited patiently for me all these years, and I need to do that for myself, to make the circle complete.

A friend of mine, a man in his eighties, told me recently, "I envy you, Troy. You have plenty of time to do everything you want in life."

There was a time I would have looked at sixty (coming up, but not here yet!) with horror, when I would have believed that number meant my life was almost done. But I've put away those fears and my regrets. I'm moving excitedly into the future, because now I know the future can be whatever I dream.

I've gone back to Whisper Mountain. We haven't sold a single lot since I left for Peaceful Valley Farm, but Charlie's parents built a retirement cabin there on a high ridge with a ten-mile view. It's their part-time home, and a gift to their children. I go to the cabin often when they are in Texas and the mountain is empty, to sit on the porch and listen to the silence. I had forgotten, in those terrible years, what a gorgeous place Whisper Mountain is. Often I read on that porch, or I write, or I draw. Whisper Mountain is a place to find your soul.

"Troy doesn't mind driving thirty miles for the perfect sunset," Charlie once explained to a friend who wondered why I was heading out so late.

Of course I don't. Why would I? It took me thirty years of hard work and determination to find a perfect place for my family. What's a thirty-minute drive compared to that?

EVEN THOUGH MY INDIVIDUALITY FEELS SWEET

KNOWING PERFECTION

I LISTEN FOR THE ANSWERS FROM ABOVE.

GOOD FINDS THE SWEET GIVER.

Post Hill Press in Nashville, Tennessee, has published a twentieth anniversary edition of Marshall's *Kiss of God*. It is available in paperback and e-book. Marshall's second book, *A Good Kiss* (Pocket Books), is available as an e-book.

To learn more about Troy & Sons, please visit our website at www.troyandsons.com.

SUGGESTED READING

Here's a list of the magazines, websites, and books that helped with my research for this book. I highly recommend them all:

Mountain Spirits by Joseph Earl Dabney (Bright Mountain Books, Asheville, NC).

Moonshine by Jaime Joyce (Zenith Press, Minneapolis, MN).

"A Visit with the Earl of Leicester" by Roger McCredie, *Capital at Play,* August 2014 (www.capitalatplay.com).

"The Forrest Jarrett Story: A Madison County Prequel," "Mama Jarrett and the Marshall Depot," and "Forrest Jarrett, Railroad Pistol-Toter" by Rob Neufield, the Read on WNC (www.thereadonwnc.ning.com).

ACKNOWLEDGMENTS

Thank you, Bret Witter and Elizabeth Butler-Witter, for the endless days and hours spent working to bring this book together.

I love the way our lives fall like dominos if you let them. Thanks to Dub Cornett for including me in a *Variety* magazine event, where I met Sean Herman, a young actor, writer, and director, who invited me to his film event at a Soho art gallery. It was there I met Abe Kasbo, a Syrian immigrant who didn't drink yet fell in love with my story. He in turn introduced me to my literary agent, Peter McGuigan at Foundry Media. Peter introduced me to the genius writer Bret Witter and my publisher, Carrie Thornton at Dey Street Books/HarperCollins. Marshall is right. "To love is to live." That loving opens all kinds of doors.

I would like to give special thanks to Mary Ann Uritis, our sons' pediatrician and my dear friend. Without your help the boys would not have stayed nearly as healthy, allowing me time to pursue my dream. Your delicious dinners fed our spirits, too.

Also, special thanks to Jerry and Jaynan Ball, who have been such a constant support in all our lives. What would I have done without my dear mother, who I just lost this year. She made our daily lives so much better with her delicious cooking and ever-present love.

I cherish the memories that Chris Martin of Coldplay has given us. We never would have dreamed that Marshall would be allowed to touch the world through his words or the love he inspires. Thank you, Dr. Habib, for the introduction to Chris. Both of you have brightened Marshall's world and ours, too.

I could not have survived the tough years that we faced after 2008 without my girlfriends. They saw me through dark days and lifted me up when I needed it most. Rosie, Carol, Aan, Joan Marie, Karen, Jennifer, Nancy, and Joan, you are my rocks and have done a good job of keeping me tethered to reality, too.

Jean Claude, thank you for bringing art back into my life and for your generous spirit. I look forward to continuing to bring focus to the love found in art, music, and words, as Marshall plans his Taccirring.

Without Marshall's steady calm presence instructing me and encouraging me, this book might never have been written. He has been the greatest inspiration in my life, besides my father. Marshall's words remind me always what is true, and that is: love kills fear, love is life, love is all.

Lastly, I want to thank Charlie, my dear husband, for his tender devotion to our family. Your love has gotten us all through some very difficult times, and I know no one could have done it better. We all thank you.

ABOUT THE AUTHORS

TROY BALL is the founder and principal owner of Asheville Distilling Company in Asheville, North Carolina, makers of Troy & Sons Platinum whiskey, Troy & Sons Oak Reserve, and Blonde whiskey. Troy & Sons Platinum recently received a gold medal for moonshine, the highest possible rating. Troy & Sons moonshine is also available in many Disney resorts. In 2004, Troy cofounded the Thoughtful House Center for Children in Austin, Texas, which has recently changed its name to the Johnson Center for Child Health and Development. Today, the center sees over 2,500 children with autism and spectrum disorders and coordinates international medical research studies. Troy lives outside Asheville, North Carolina, with her husband, Charlie, and two of their three grown sons, Marshall and Coulton, who have special needs.

BRET WITTER is the writer of eight *New York Times* bestsellers, including the #1 bestsellers *Dewey* and *The Monuments Men*. He lives in Decatur, Georgia.